TRINITY

A Story of Deep Delight

First published in 2017

by COLUMBA PRESS

23 Merrion Square

Dublin 2, Ireland

www.columba.ie

ISBN: 978 1 78218 349 5

Set in Linux Libertine 12/16

Cover and book design by Alba Esteban | Columba Press

Printed by ScandBook, Sweden

TRINITY

A Story of Deep Delight

ANNE MARIE MONGOVEN O.P.

columba press

To Rita Claire Dorner, O.P.,
friend, sister, and companion on the way

Contents

INTRODUCTION

Trinity: A Story of Deep Delight

As I was writing this book, I found that Robert Penn Warren's words from *Audubon* reflected my own "deep delight" in exploring the reality of Trinity-Love:

> *Tell me a story:*
> *In this century, and moment, of mania...*
> *Make it a story of great distances, and starlight...*
> *Tell me a story of deep delight.*

It is always a delight, a surprise, to be loved. The yearning to be loved seems to be a natural human characteristic. It is not that people seek to be loved by everyone, but people find great joy in being loved by someone whom they love. A mutual love-relationship transforms each of the lovers. It fills them with delight, frees them from self-preoccupation, and gives them a purpose for being. What is the source of this yearning that leads to happiness for friends and lovers?

This book explores the primary and the ultimate source of love – God as Trinity. It focuses on Trinitarian relationships and what these relationships mean in our lives. Christians believe that God – the Holy Trinity – is Love itself and the source of all love. Some theologians describe the Trinity as a "Communion of Love," a communion of three persons whose mutual love is so intimate that the three are one. This is not an arithmetical puzzle. It is a description of the nature of love relationships. The love within the Trinity sets it apart from all other love relationships because in Trinitarian love the lovers are intimately and fully one in their love.

Relating through love is the essence of God. Loving always implies relationship, for the one who loves needs a beloved, and the lover and beloved are drawn to one another through their mutual love. As Creator, God created humans in the divine "image and likeness," thereby giving us the possibility of loving and accepting love as God does. Only Christians profess God to be a Trinity of love.

This book attempts to describe the living font of all love, the Trinity. It examines the nature of the relationships among the Father, the Son, and the Holy Spirit, and the relationship of Trinity with all of Creation. This book is about a passionate and fruitful God whose creativity in loving brings all that is into existence.

Most Christians, with the exception of mystics, have not described their experience of God in terms of a surge of love or affection for Trinity. People may say that they love God, but this love is usually not characterised as passionate or liberating. The reason for this may be that for generations, the nature of Trinity has been inaccessible to many of us.

Initially, in the early centuries of the Church, the

doctrine of the Trinity was full of vitality, at the very centre of Christian faith. St Gregory of Nyssa tells us that in the late 4th Century, the Trinity was so significant to people that they argued in the market about the nature and relationships of the Trinity. That no longer happens today. Yet, Trinity was, and still is, the heart of Church life, prayer, and belief. For centuries, the knowledge of the Trinity captured peoples' imagination and led them not only to Baptism (*"In the name of the Father, and the Son, and the Holy Spirit"*) but also to martyrdom. Great scholars like Augustine and Thomas Aquinas wrote eloquently and with passion about the Trinity.

However, interest in Trinity declined, and by the time of the Council of Trent (1545-1563) with the separation of the Christian Churches, the description of and teaching about the Holy Trinity began to change. It became somewhat static, arid, sometimes unintelligible or irrelevant to most Christians. Being Trinity means that the loving God, traditionally named Father, Son, and Holy Spirit, is one in an intimate love relationship with itself, but Christians need to rediscover the truth that Trinity also lives in a deep love relationship with humans and with all of Creation.

I write about Trinity because the mystery of God is so embracing, enlightening, and enabling that I cannot *not* write about it. The Trinity to which my community of faith and I are intimately and passionately related is the font of human happiness and the model of human life at its best Trinity is the one God who embraces itself and all of Creation with Love. As Trinity, God looks lovingly toward humankind and to all of Creation whom it invites into its heart even as it embraces itself.

That God is Trinity is Christians' reply to questions like "Who is God?" I think that Christians today have a right to know how their Church, from its heart and from its head, responds to the question: "What do we know about God as Trinity?" We as Church say "God is love," (1Jn 4:8) and our yearning to be loved and to love is directly related to the loving God who creates us.

Sometimes my friends ask me, "What effect does Trinity have in our lives?" They believe in Trinity but most of them probably put their faith in Jesus, not recognising Trinity as the source of Jesus' love, or not seeing God the Father as the one who so loved the world that "he gave his only Son " (Jn. 3:16). This is because people recognise Jesus as human and feel they can have a relationship with the human Saviour. They may recognise Trinity as godly or loving but do not realise that they themselves actually share in Trinity's godliness and are called by Trinity to love.

My response to the question, "Why do you write about Trinity?" is that Trinity is itself the Mystery of Love. Trinity creates out of love. Trinity sent Jesus, the Son, out of love, and Jesus called on the Holy Spirit to be the source and enabler of our love. Being loved by Love itself enables me to love and gives me fresh life every day. It is the source of my deepest happiness.

Trinity is the most significant answer we can give to

the question, "Who is God?" That God is Trinity is Jesus' foundational preaching and teaching. All questions about faith or God or human life or Creation relate to our understanding of who God is and the nature of our consequent relationship with God. Every moral question, every prayer, every relationship, every hope for the future, every happy moment in life has its own particular spirit because of our conception of the nature of God.

The Uniqueness of this Book

This book is primarily a meditation on Trinity as God who is Love. It is a pastoral writing that continually reflects not only on the nature and love of God but also on the possible implications of Trinity's relationship with humans.

Trinity: A Story of Deep Delight offers a reflection on Trinity and each of the Trinitarian persons by examining images of Trinity from Church prayer, hymns, and especially from biblical, theological, liturgical, and spirituality writings. Since Karl Rahner, S.J., (1904-1984) published his book, *The Trinity* (1967), a massive rethinking of every aspect of Trinitarian theology has taken place and this rethinking has renewed the theology of Trinity. This renewed theology brings spirit and life to our understanding of and relationship with Trinity.

I hope this book may lead you, the reader, to love more fully, love God, love your neighbour, love yourself, love the universe and everything in it. If we are open to Trinity's love, we may be transformed by it so that we become ever more loving and loveable in our daily lives. The essence of Trinity is the grandest of love relationships and is the foundation of a spirituality of loving. I hope this *Story of Deep Delight* will invite you to discover for yourself how you personally relate to Trinity-Love.

The Development of this Story of Deep Delight

Chapter One, *The Mystery of the Trinity,* introduces the theme of this book, that of *relationship* – the relationships within Trinity and the relationships between Trinity and all of Creation, particularly with humankind. Its basic premise is that all things are related, or as Pope Francis says in *Laudato Si,* "Everything is connected".

Chapter Two, *The Mystery of the Loving Father,* reviews the significance of traditional images of God as Father and Creator. It also reintroduces Augustine's triad of images for Trinity: *Lover, Beloved, and Love.* Because of serious questions about using gender exclusive images for God, some recently developed alternative images are also considered.

Chapter Three reflects on the Mystery of the Beloved Son as Messiah, a Jewish title and an early Jewish interpretation of Jesus' mission. Images of Jesus as God, and as the Father's Beloved Son are found in early Christian hymns. The Philippian hymn was written and subsequently inserted into an epistle. In the epistle to the Colossians, the images of Christ as cosmic Lord pouring love into the universe presents Christ as above and beyond all of Creation. Reflection on images for Christ and Trinity in these two hymns may lead readers to understand the Christian community's relationship with Jesus and Trinity during the 1st Century of the Christian era. Chapter Three considers nouns, titles, and images with which the faith community prayed during the century of Jesus death-resurrection-glorification.

Chapter Four, *The Mystery of Spirit-Love,* reflects on dynamic images of the Spirit. Not only are biblical images considered, but the chapter also includes a reflection on images for the Spirit in two classic medieval hymns, the *Veni Creator Spiritus* and *Veni Sancte Spiritus,* so we may consider what images and concepts the medieval Church used to name and relate to the Holy Spirit.

Chapter Five, *Being One in Love,* is a commentary on Trinity's relationship to humankind. We know Trinity is in itself one in love, as St Augustine states – the Lover, the Beloved, and the Unifying Love. But what is the nature of Trinity's love, and how does Trinity relate to us and we to Trinity? Trinity's relationship to humankind is one of friendship-love. This relationship, like all friendship relationships, is a free and shared love through which the human person is transformed and becomes more and more Trinitarian and loving.

Through reflection on chapters 13-17 in John's Gospel, with particular emphasis on chapter 15, the *Abide in Me* discourse, the reader may discover a renewed view of what it means to describe Trinity as a full, free, and creative friend with individuals and communities. It is through Jesus' own words in John's Gospel that we examine what friendship with Trinity is like. In Chapter 15, Jesus describes what friendship is, and as a result of that description we have a clear understanding of what Jesus means when he refers to his followers as friends, and what it means for us to live in a relationship of friendship with Trinity.

Deep delight emerges from our own realisation that Trinity's love for us really matters. Our yearning for love is fulfilled when we recognise that we are already Trinity's beloveds, and that every one of us is loved fully, passionately, and fruitfully.

ONE

THE MYSTERY OF TRINITY

The Sign of the Trinity

A young Buddhist woman named Nooria, while preparing to become a Catholic, asked her initiation community, "When are we going to learn the sign of the Trinity?" At first we did not know what Nooria's question meant, so someone asked, "What do you mean by the sign of the Trinity?" Nooria replied, "You know, that prayer where you say some words and move your hand from your forehead to your heart, and then to each of your shoulders!"

Obviously, Nooria was referring to what Catholics call "The Sign of the Cross," but Nooria enlightened all of us by naming that prayer "The Sign of the Trinity". As a Trinitarian prayer, both the gesture and the words naming the Trinity "the Father, the Son, and the Holy Spirit" proclaim the heart of Christian faith. Christian life is not only a continuing response to the redemptive love of Christ expressed through the Cross, but also a response to the constant and transforming love of the Triune God for all people, each and every one, throughout all of time.

Jews, Muslims, and Christians all believe there is only one God, but only Christians profess that the one God is both one and triune. Identifying God as both "one and triune" is puzzling and seemingly contradictory to many people. Sometimes theologians respond to the question of how God can be both one and triune when they say that the Trinity is a "mystery". The word "mystery" may seem too simple a solution unless we recognise that theologically "mystery" means that the reality is far too profound for humankind to ever understand it fully.

A theological mystery is a reality about which we can always know more. It is infinite, unfathomable, and immeasurable in scope and depth. Naming a concept a *mystery* does not imply that humankind knows nothing about the reality. On the contrary, we can always know more about the mystery because it is profoundly beyond human comprehension. We Christians do not and cannot fully understand the mystery of who God is even though every theological mystery continues to reveal itself. New insights emerge and old and familiar concepts continue to develop. Trinity is a Holy Mystery.

Unfolding the Mystery of Love

The sentence "God is love" (1Jn 4: 8), tells us everything we need to know about God. It is an early Christian concept recorded in the first epistle of John. It is a three-word sentence about which we can still ask, "Is there any other sentence in the English language that reveals so much about the Triune God or about Trinity's relationship to humankind?"

The words "*God is love*" seem almost too familiar though they still should startle us. We have many other images of God that are more readily understandable, such as God as creator, judge, protector, but can we really imagine God as "love"? Many wonderful sentences have described God, but surely these three words, *God is love,* tell us more about God than all other images.

Human beings know from their own experience a great deal about love. We know that love is always relational. This relationship implies a reciprocal action of loving. Loving expresses itself in a compassionate and generous way and ordinarily develops over time. It transforms the participants by relating them in a love that reorders their priorities in life. It presumes a lover and a beloved who are freely related through mutual love. Ordinarily it expresses itself in a family, a marriage, or a friendship.

The Triune God is not a solitary being. Trinity is one divine love-relationship of three unique beings that theologians describe as persons. In this relationship, the shared love is so full and compelling that the three persons are truly one in mutual love.

St Augustine describes the relationship among the three persons in the Trinity by referring to them relationally as "the Lover," "the Beloved", and "Love," or the one who is the bond of love among the three. The Father is the Lover,

the Son is the Beloved, and the Holy Spirit is Spirit-Love –
the bonding love that unites the three as one God.

A lover cannot exist without a beloved. A beloved
cannot exist without a lover. Both lover and beloved need
a bond of love to exist as one Love. This identification of
the mutual love relationship within God distinguishes the
Christian vision of God from that of all other religious
faiths. No other religious community recognises God as
diverse and equal persons living in a communion of love.
No other religious faith proclaims unequivocally "God is
love." When Christians ask, "Who is God?" the response is
that God is Trinity, three unique persons bound together
in a union of love. This Triune God is a communion of love
who reaches out in an embrace of love to all that is, was,
or ever will be.

To say "God is love" is to say that God is loving. God's
becoming human or incarnate in Jesus is an act of love for
all of Creation. Jesus is the human expression of divine
love. St John describes God's self-giving love in his Gospel
by saying that "God so loved the world that he gave his
only Son" (Jn 3: 16). The purpose of this gift was to free
humankind from the burden of its own selfishness and
sin. Jesus, the incarnate Son of God, is the most profound
expression of God's love.

If people want to know what God's love is like, they
may examine Jesus' life to see how love lives. They may
learn from Jesus by listening to his word, observing his
relationships with others, including the sick and the blind

and the deaf, the poor, the marginalised, the suffering, and all women, men, and children. As the Son of God, Jesus revealed the nature of God in his human life.

Observe how Jesus relates to children, to Mary Magdalene, the woman at the well, the sisters of Lazarus, the chief priests, the Pharisees, his own apostles, and his mother. As the incarnation of Love itself, the incarnate Son of God made visible the love that lives within Trinity and the love that God invites humankind to share with all of Creation. God calls us to live in love as the Trinity does.

God does not live in isolation. Trinity is Love itself, reaching out in grace, compassion, and love to humankind and all of Creation. The love of God begets love. All of Creation is an expression of God's love. Humankind is the self-conscious progeny of God, created in the likeness of God, created to be loving as God is loving. Through the Creation of humankind God graced the cosmos with divine love.

Trinity is Essentially Relational

Life within Trinity is never static. God's love is full of energy, freely and decisively given. God's love moves out from Trinity through and into all of Creation, including humankind, and back to the God who initiated the love cycle. Words cannot begin to describe the fullness of love that God has for all that is. The divine love is so embracing and enlivening that it is central to every human life, even when humankind does not recognise it.

It was Jesus who named the three persons in a relational

way when he named the Father, the Son, and the Holy Spirit as the one God (Mt 28: 19). "Father" is a word that describes a special relationship. In order to be a father, one must relate to a child like a father, one who gives or is the source of new life. A child may recognise an adult as its father, and the adult may be a father through adoption, not only through physical generation. Human beings are adopted children of God, for we do not share the same divine nature as God.

As God's love is relational, so is human loving. As Trinity is relational in essence, God chooses to live in an intimate love relationship with all created reality, especially with humankind. The focus of God's relationship, both within the Trinity and with all created reality, is loving.

St Thomas Aquinas, when dying, described his extraordinarily profound theological writings as "straw". In doing so, St Thomas acknowledged that the marvellous insights given to him through study, prayer, a holy life, the Church, and the Holy Spirit, while profound and beautiful, could not compare with the truth and beauty of God. Human words and concepts are always inadequate for describing such a divine being. Trinity is a mystery of Love.

The simple sentence in John's first epistle that tells us "God is love," reveals that God is relational. Love is always relational, but everything that is relational is not always love. In the realm of possibility a god could relate, as humans too often do, with vindictiveness, negativity, abuse, or overwhelming power. But Trinity is love and is by nature good, and as St Thomas Aquinas noted, it is the nature of goodness to overflow. The goodness of Trinity is naturally outgoing. The phrase "communion of love" describes Trinity as one in the fullness of love and communal in that oneness. All are one who lives in the fullness of God's grace. Trinity, living as the fullness of love, is at the same time reaching out lovingly to humankind and receiving and accepting our love. One could say that God breathes out divine love and breathes in human love.

God's inner life is relational and loving. Marvel of marvels, Trinity extends divine life freely and lovingly to humankind and all of Creation. Trinity's love is profuse and passionate with the same fullness as the love that flourishes within Trinity itself. All that Trinity has created is an expression of God's goodness in love.

Christians and Jews ordinarily interpret the biblical statement that says God created humankind in the image and likeness of the Divine (Gn. 1: 27) to mean that Trinity created humankind to be like God. Trinity calls humankind to be like itself, to embrace freely and decisively with living love all of created reality, especially other humans. Trinity created humankind to be one people, one in love with Trinity, one in love with one another, and one in love with all of Creation. That, I believe, is the Kingdom of Love that Jesus preached. Trinity's love expresses itself in abundant love poured out to all of Creation, from the cosmos to the butterfly to humankind. We have been called not only to justice, but also to love. "Justice is love's absolute minimum," said the United States Bishops in *Sharing the Light of Faith,* the National Catechetical Directory. We are called to the fullness of love, and the best we can do in naming God is to say, "God is Love".

The Mystery of God as Trinity is beyond human comprehension. Therefore, we need to reflect on how Jesus spoke about his Father and the Holy Spirit and relate to them through Jesus. He introduced the Father and the Spirit through his sermons and his discourses. Jesus always spoke of the Father as loving, providential, protective, and steadfast in his relationship with his people. Later in this chapter we will reflect on Jesus' *Sermon on the Mount* and note how full it is with references to his loving Father.

In his most intimate conversations with his apostles, Jesus spoke of Trinity as intimately, ecstatically, and passionately in love with all of Creation. Trinity was to him not simply a God to be adored but a God to be loved because this God is love. Trinity is love; Trinity is the beginning and the end, the *alpha* and *omega.*

Jesus' words tell us that he knew the Father and the Spirit were with him. When Philip asked him, "Lord, show us the father, and we will be satisfied," Jesus said to him, "Have I been with you all this time, Philip, and you still do not know me? Whoever has seen me has seen the Father" (Jn 14:9). Jesus professed to have an intimate Trinitarian relationship of love, in this case particularly with the Father. In his life, through his words, Jesus announced that he and the Father were one. He assumed a Trinitarian reality in his words about himself and his mission. It is Jesus who revealed to the Church that God is Trinity, a triune communion of love. It is through Jesus' relationship with Trinity, expressed through words and actions, that the Church came to know Trinity. What Jesus revealed about his relationship with Trinity was handed on to his disciples and from their generation to generations through the centuries until today and into the days to come.

Though many scholars and many saints have tried to do so, no one can ever fully describe the Triune God. In the history of the Church, both mystics and theologians, men and women, have written about Trinity insofar as they know Trinity. The Triune God is not simply an intellectual concept that has no relationship to ordinary life. Experiencing Trinity as a communion of pure love in which we have been given a part in our ordinary daily lives can lead us to recognise that Divinity is everywhere. All that is, all of Creation, mirrors Trinity. The structure of every reality is Trinitarian. Every human is Trinitarian because every person is relational as the Triune God is relational.

Through ordinary daily human life, people may experience Trinity's grace and be aware of its presence. Once Christians begin to look anew at what Jesus taught about Trinity, we may marvel and begin to live the reality of Trinity's life and love among us.

To live a Trinitarian life means to live actively and consciously in a reciprocal relationship of love with the Triune God and with all of Creation, especially with our human sisters and brothers. We do not need to know words that describe the reality we love. However, sometimes, perhaps even momentarily, we may recognise the Divine Love among us, actively loving in and through our lives, and almost inarticulately we may say in our hearts, "Yes, thank you". "O Trinity! Teach us to love!"

The one thing we know unequivocally about the Triune God is that the essence of Trinity is relatedness through love. The love of God soars within Trinity and reaches out to humankind to draw it within its own life of love. God is our Friend.

Humankind is Essentially Relational

As in Trinity, so in human beings, relationship is the heart of life. Human beings are relational people and, like Trinity, we relate to the entire universe. It is as relational beings that we are in the image and likeness of Trinity. St Paul knew we were created to love, and he described this love in a letter to the Corinthians:

> *Love is patient; love is kind; love is not envious or boastful or arrogant or rude. It does not insist on its own way; it is not irritable or resentful; it does not rejoice in wrongdoing, but rejoices in the truth. It bears all things, believes all things, hopes all things, endures all things. Love never ends ... now faith, hope, and love abide, these three; and the greatest of these is love.*
>
> *– 1 Cor. 13:4-13*

Trinity's love never ends. In the Hebrew Scriptures, Trinity's love is frequently described as "steadfast". Trinity's love is constant. It supports us in our weakness. It is fatherly and motherly, sisterly and brotherly. It is the love of a friend, a very close friend.

However, we differ, in that our relationships are not always loving. The love of human beings can end. It is never totally whole. That is not to say that it is worthless, for our love is the greatest gift we can give. Yet, our love has been touched by darkness. We can be abusive, mean, arrogant, or possessive. Humans can and do love deeply, but humans live in a world where Evil is present, touching each one of us, inviting us to be unloving, selfish, envious. Trinity's gracious love overcomes all evil, but we are still subject to temptation, to seek our own good above the good of others.

Loving relationships sustain and give hope for the future. These relationships are the spokes of the wheel that give individuals and communities their own uniqueness, as well as their own strength and freedom. The act of loving unites individuals and communities. It gives people desire and energy to begin each new day. To be loved, to love, and to know love is the very heart of human life.

The human experience of love is interaction between persons who are spouses, parents, siblings, and friends. Their shared love alters the life of both lovers and beloveds. It enables each person to develop his or her own gifts and identity. Participating in human love relationships frees people to open themselves to divine love. Conversely, the response to divine love leads one to love all that is.

To love or not to love is not simply an intellectual decision. It is a human decision that involves the totality of the deciding person. This decision will both change and perhaps radically alter each loving person. The experience of human love prepares one for the recognition and acceptance of divine love.

Every human love relationship is unique because of the uniqueness of each person in the shared love. Relationships of love emerge in varied forms such as family love, friendship love, married love. Family love may grow through daily contact with the people who are members of the family. The love relationship of parents sets the environment for whatever relationships develop within the family. The greatest gift parents can give their children is the strength of the parents' mutual love. Parents who create a culture of kindness, generosity, respect, even reverence for one another and for family, give unspoken direction to the way in which family members develop or relate to one another.

Friendship is a deeply significant form of love. Friends share joy, wonder, grief, and happiness with one another and make the other's burden lighter. They laugh at one another's *faux pas*, and dull the pain of larger mistakes. Friends support or may even chastise the other occasionally, but always lovingly. Some friendships begin in childhood and last throughout a lifetime. In the course of life, new friends bring new joys.

One cannot begin to search for a friend. Friendships are surprise gifts that emerge without planning. Many friends are both complementary and diverse in nature. As persons begin to know one another, a friendship may form quite unexpectedly. The essential characteristic of friendship is a growing and deeper affection over time. Once formed, friendships transform those who enter into such a relationship. Maintaining a friendship involves fidelity in affection. Friendship can be a costly relationship because it includes an embracing and a giving of oneself in love to another. Friendship is an experience of delight that deepens the mutual affection. Love gives birth to love. Love strengthens love. Love calls forth from each friend solicitude, kindness, generosity.

The love of friendship gives new life to both friends. When one lives in a relationship of friendship, a deep abiding joy undergirds all of life. Whatever difficulty a friend faces, she/he knows she/he does not face it alone. Friendship bestows confidence. It frees us to speak of our private joys and of our private sorrows as well. Friendship enables us to recognise that we are never alone. The love and confidence of a friend is always present as grace.

Somehow it sounds presumptuous to describe Trinity as "friendly." Perhaps the "loving" Trinity or the "forgiving" Trinity, or even the "fatherly" or "motherly" Trinity would not sound so bold. "Friendly" as an adjective to describe a human relationship with the Triune God may sound disrespectful to some. Can Trinity be a friend? Is Trinity our friend?

It is interesting to note that the Second Vatican Council in its *Dogmatic Constitution On Divine Revelation*, which many theologians consider to be the most significant and transformative of its documents, includes the following statement:

> "It pleased God, in his goodness and wisdom, to reveal himself and to make known the mystery of his will (Eph. 1:9), which was that people can draw near to the Father, through Christ, the Word made flesh, in the Holy Spirit, and thus become sharers in the divine nature (See Eph. 2:18, 2Pet. 1:4). By this revelation, then, the invisible God from the fullness of his love, addresses men and women as his friends (see Ex. 33:13; Jn 15:14-15), and lives among them (see Bar. 3:38), in order to invite and receive them into his own company" (art. 2).

God is our friend.

Everything is Related

The great Genesis myth of Creation begins with the astonishing story of the Creation of Heaven and Earth, of all that is. It is primarily a story of love, goodness, and wonder, though there is sin in it also. Poetic in form, sublime in tone, Genesis introduces God without an introduction. The story begins "in the beginning," although even before the beginning God was already present. According to the author or authors of this story, only a "formless void" existed, a formless void covered with darkness. Suddenly "a wind from God swept over the face of the waters," and with that wind, Creation began.

God said, "Let there be light," and light came and God separated the light from the darkness. God called the light Day, and the darkness Night. On continuing days God called forth the dome of the sky and separated the waters under the dome from the waters over the dome, and the dry land appeared. With a word from God the plants yielding seeds and fruit trees of every kind began to be.

God put lights in the dome of the sky and a bright light for day, a dimmer light for night, great sea monsters, and winged birds of every kind – all came into being in response to God's Word. God spoke, and cattle and creeping things and wild animals of every kind came to be. And God saw that all that was made was good. After all the plants and animals, sea and sky, land and mountains were created, God said,

> "Let us make humankind in our image, according to our likeness, and let them have dominion over the fish of the sea, and over the birds of the air, and over the cattle, and over all the wild animals of the Earth, and over every creeping thing that creeps upon the Earth."

God created humankind as an image of the divine. Male and female, God created them both in the divine image.

God blessed them, and God said to them, "Be fruitful and multiply, and fill the Earth and subdue it; and have dominion over the fish of the sea and over the birds of the air and over every living thing that moves upon the Earth". God said, "See, I have given you every plant yielding seed that is upon the face of all the Earth, and every tree with seed in its fruit; you shall have them for food. And to every beast of the Earth, and to every bird of the air, and to everything that creeps on the Earth, everything that has the breath of life, I have given every green plant for food" And it was so. God saw everything that he had made, and indeed, it was very good. And there was evening and there was morning, the sixth day.

– Genesis 1:28-31

The biblical story of God's Creation of Heaven and Earth is a wondrous story, poetical in form, gracious in spirit. It lifts humankind to an intimate relationship with the divine. The authors recognised that human beings, created in God's image, were given responsibility for all that God created. Humankind was asked to continue the Creation process, to be co-creators with God.

The Genesis story of Creation is not a scientific account of how created reality came to be. It is a human interpretation drawn from human experience, faith commitment, and the limited scientific knowledge at the time it was written. It is an epic myth in harmony with present day expositions of an evolving universe over billions of years. Truth emerges from human experience influenced by religious faith. The biblical story of Creation describes the relationships of all creatures to God as Creator.

In his encyclical *On Care for Our Common Home*, Pope Francis reminds us again and again that "everything is connected". Everything is connected and we as Trinitarian people are invited to keep the relationship strong and loving. In this encyclical Pope Francis wrote a stunning, a surprising sentence. Very few authors would dare to say as Pope Francis did, "I wish to address every person living on this planet" (art. 2). Most writers never think of such an all-encompassing readership. That Pope Francis could write such a sentence indicates his profound concern for life on Earth, and his recognition that the indifference, abuse, and plunder of our planet are primarily results of our human action. In this encyclical, Pope Francis emphasises his concern for the whole cosmos, which he terms "Our Common Home".

Pope Francis reminds his readers that humankind has inflicted irreparable harm on all of Creation. He indicates that although the cosmos may not yet be near death, many of its living species are already extinct or endangered. All of created reality suffers in some way from the effects of human misuse, destruction, and carelessness. And the process threatens the lives of the people who are already in great need, those who live in poverty.

Pope Francis' theme – that "everything is connected" – relates directly to the renewed theological theme that describes both the Mystery of Trinity and the mystery of humankind, "Everything is related." It is not only the Triune God who is one in intimate relationship. Humankind is related not only to its own species. All created reality relates or connects in some way to humankind and ultimately to the Triune God. Nothing is extraneous or isolated from any other created reality because we all are related through God's loving creativity.

Environmentalism or human responsibility for the stewardship of Creation is not a new concept. It began in the beginning. There have been people on Earth, at different times and in various places, who expressed deep appreciation of and care for the environmental character of life. Over millennia, different peoples and varied cultures recognised in religious language the sacredness of Creation. Native Americans, for example, are known for their recognition and preservation of the sacredness of Earth.

In the 20th and 21st Centuries, as more and more natural species were eliminated from the Earth or endangered, the balance of nature was upset. As climate changes drastically, societies begin to recognise that if humanity itself is to survive, human stewardship of Creation is a not an optional activity but a necessity. The 2015 Paris Conference on environmental changes brought together participants and representatives of over two hundred nations who issued a public declaration of their concern for the environment.

There is no created reality that is not connected with all other created reality. The U.S. Endangered Species Act notes that due to global warming, polar bears are threatened by extinction. The warming climate on Earth, caused primarily by the use of fossil fuels thousands of miles from the Arctic Circle, is changing the environment of the polar bears. Their habitat can no longer support their needs.

The Monarch butterfly is another example of an endangered species. The Monarchs' summer breeding habitat requires milkweed plants growing in North America's back yards, on farmland, and on highway borders and trails. This habitat changed drastically as farmers, local government agencies, and individuals removed the milkweed plants which were perceived as a nuisance. As a consequence, the U.S. Center for Biological Diversity reported that in 2016, the Monarch population had declined by 78% from the population highs of the mid-1990s. The polar bear and the Monarch butterfly are only two of many species in danger due to our lack of care for "our common home".

Who is the God we Love?

The question: "What or Who is the Mystery of Trinity?" is a question that Christians have been studying, preaching, and proclaiming for two millennia, so it seems reasonable to expect that Christians could find information about the Trinity in the Bible. The Bible is, as Karl Rahner, S.J., wrote, "the Church's book". It is the Church's book because the Hebrew Scriptures were handed on to us by Jesus and the apostolic Church, and the Christian Scriptures were written as witness to the life, death, resurrection, glorification of Jesus, and the life of the apostolic Church.

The Bible is the sacred book of Christians because it tells us of God's steadfast love for us as well as stories of our holy women and men. It is the Church's Book because the Church approved it, preserved it, and still proclaims it. The Church incorporates biblical writings into its daily, weekly, and seasonal prayer. It recognises the Hebrew Scriptures (or Old Testament) as inspired books. The Hebrew Scriptures are the sacred writings of the Jewish people, writings that Jesus loved and lived by during his time on Earth. The Bible, including both Hebrew and Christian Scriptures, is so sacred that it is called the "Word of God." The God of the Hebrew Scriptures is the same God as the God of the New Testament or Christian Scriptures. The God of the Bible is the God Christians love and proclaim as "our God".

Since Christians identify Jesus the Christ as the Son of God, and since we commit ourselves to that God as Trinity, one might expect that the Scriptures speak often of the Trinity, but the word *Trinity* never appears in the Bible. Not ever. The understanding that God is Trinity was given to us through the preaching of Jesus. Why did Jesus not speak of Trinity?

Jesus did speak of Trinity but never used the word "Trinity" to name the God of whom he spoke. Often when he preached Jesus told his followers about the Father or the Spirit. He identified himself and his disciples identified him as God's Son. Jesus went so far as to say to Philip who asked him how they could see the Father to whom Jesus said he was going, "Philip, have you been with me so long and still you do not know me? He who sees me sees the Father" (Jn 14:9).

Jesus is the symbol of the Father and the Spirit. The people who are the Church are the symbols of the Church. Church is the symbol both of Christ and of the people who are the Church. All realities are encountered through their symbols. It is through their symbols that every reality is made present.

Symbols speak to our imagination. While Individuals and communities are both intensive and evocative symbols, their words and actions are also symbolic. American people think they know Abraham Lincoln through the artefacts that make him present to them and also through his words and actions. The Gettysburg Address speaks to Americans as Lincoln as does the Lincoln Memorial sculpture. Every symbol has more or less significance insofar as that which it makes present in the world has meaning.

Binding all together as one in love is what the Church is and does. The Bible when speaking of faith does not mean a blind acceptance of something difficult to believe or understand. The persons or communities of "faith" in the Scriptures are those who freely and willingly commit themselves to the God of love.

The Scriptures share the story of men and women, faithful and unfaithful, who have gone before us. The biblical stories give us insight into the nature of the Israelite-Jewish and Christian communities. Who was the God of the Israelites? That God was and is a steadfastly loving and protective God. This God was also a warrior God, faithful to a sometimes unfaithful and idolatrous people.

Jesus named the Christian God "Father," "Son," and "Holy Spirit". The apostle John, Jesus' beloved disciple, wrote late in the 1st Century that *God is Love* (Jn 4:8). Both responses are true. The God of Jesus is the Father, the Son, and the Holy Spirit, and that God is Love.

The New Testament gives us the narrative of the birth, baptism, passion, death, resurrection and glorification of Jesus. It proclaims Jesus to be the Messiah inaugurating the reign of God on Earth. Like the Hebrew Scriptures, the New Testament shares with its communities and individuals stories of great love that led to martyrdom, as well as stories that led to unfaithfulness and death. The New Testament offers us early hymns that the Church still sings today. It offers descriptions of the lives and values of early communities, so that later communities can feed upon and grow with the Word of God.

The writings of the entire Bible testify with deep love

and awe that God is Trinity. The Hebrew Scriptures do not speak of God as Trinity, except perhaps through stories, prayers, proverbs or hymns that some commentators think are "footprints" of the Trinity. Through these "footprints" Christians read into the Hebrew Scriptures what they as Christians learned from Jesus about God. Understandably, Jewish readers often find this form of reading offensive.

The fact that the word "Trinity" never appears in the Bible does not imply that the Bible does not speak its most significant truth of who God is. Jesus, the incarnate Word of God, introduces us to the great mystery of the Triune God through images and stories that emerge from his own intimate relationship with Trinity. The Bible speaks of the Triune God through Jesus' words, without using an abstract concept like "Trinity". The Bible speaks of the Triune God as the Church does – through story, symbol, and ritual. The Bible is a love story, and ordinary language can never fully express divine love. But in the way Jesus speaks of the Father, the Word, and the Spirit, he tells us all we need to know. The essence of the Trinity is its relatedness. The Trinity is not only one intimately related Being, but one living, intimate, creative, passionate, and ecstatic Love.

In the New Testament, Jesus introduces his disciples to the Triune God by naming the persons of Trinity. He does so through his prayer, preaching, and stories. Jesus speaks of his relationship with the Father and the Spirit in concrete language as distinct from abstract terms. "The

Father and I are one," he says (Jn 10:30). Jesus describes his disciples' relationship with God by telling them to pray with the words, "Our Father". Jesus says, "If I do not go, the Advocate will not come". Advocate and Paraclete are Jesus' images of the Spirit to whom both the Father and the Word are intimately related. A Paraclete is one who pleads for another, a defender of the defenceless. In its prayer the Church describes the Spirit as the Lord and Giver of Life, the one who spoke through the prophets. All of these descriptions indicate a loving relationship. Jesus may never use the word "Trinity," but his words and actions reveal who the Trinity is in itself and who the Trinity is for us.

Whenever Jesus speaks of the persons of the Trinity, he describes them as different from one another. Each is unique. They are also alike in that each person is loving, compassionate, free, and dynamic. In the Gospels, God is never abstract. God is personal, taking care of the lilies of the field, forgiving an adulterous woman, telling Zacchaeus that he wants to come to his home for a meal. The Scriptures tell us through Jesus' words and actions what God is like. The Scriptures give us many pictures of Jesus and each of those "snapshots" is also a symbol of the Trinity. Our Triune God is diverse, loving, forgiving, relational, and ever-present, intervening in our lives as a loving father or mother or friend would do.

TWO

THE MYSTERY OF THE LOVING FATHER

The Bible is a Love Story

A biblical professor with whom I studied began his class each day with the same six words: "The Bible is a love story". Whatever aspect of the Sacred Scriptures we were studying, periodically, in the middle, and again near the end of a class, our professor would repeat the phrase, "The Bible is a love story".

I am sure I learned much about the Bible from Fr Sean Quinlan, but the most important thing I learned and have never forgotten is that "the Bible is a love story". This concept gives biblical readers a significant guide to understanding the many different literary forms the biblical authors used to tell the story of God and their people. The Bible is all about love. That is one reason why believers name the Bible the Word of God.

The primary story in the Bible is the story of Trinity and Trinity's love for us. This story names the living God and tells us who this God is. The name Trinity never appears in the Bible, but in naming the one God, Father,

Son, and Holy Spirit, Jesus revealed that God is triune. Jesus' revelation of the all-loving Triune God leads us, as it led his disciples, to acknowledge our relationship of love with God, with humankind, and with all created reality.

The Bible is not a science story. It is not a biography. It is not even a factual history. It is the story of the extraordinary love that God *is,* and it reveals the faithful and steadfast love through which God relates to humankind and all created reality. Through many literary forms, such as myth, poetry, genealogy, story, song, lament, proclamation, apocalypse, and letters, the Bible tells the story of God's love. Underlying these literary forms is the recognition that accepting God's love brings about a transformative experience, a new and deeper relationship with God.

The Bible is a story of both acceptance and rejection. Acceptance stories tell of relationships of love, friendship, community and family. Rejection stories tell of the darker parts of life, those moments when God cannot be found or is not sought.

Love stories tell of acceptance and relationships. Rejection stories or stories without love speak of the rift between those who might have been one in love. Rejection stories tell of destroyed relationships. Those who reject God's love may unknowingly reject their own humanness. The Bible illustrates the folly of separation and the strength of self-giving and self-accepting relationships. God's love never rejects others, and God never stops loving all that is. In the Bible, we learn that God is faithful in love. God is ecstatically loving, creative, protective, strong, friendly, communal and one. In loving, we are told that God is like a "shepherd," a "mother," a "comforter".

Throughout the Bible the Israelite, Jewish, and Christian peoples introduce God to their posterity and to central events in their communal life through images, stories, and rituals. These biblical images tell readers much about God, but each image, each story, and each ritual is limited in its description of God. Some images of God are more significant than others, but even all possible images together cannot express the fullness of God's life and love. At the same time, images, stories, and rituals do introduce humankind to God, and the closer the images are to the reality of God, the more adequately they present God. In responding to their images, stories, and rituals, the people are transformed. Every word, every story, every book in the Bible needs to be read through the prism of love.

The Image of the Creator

How can we find the words, paint the picture, sculpt the statue, or design the building that speaks adequately of the creativity and beauty of God? Nor can any one of us describe the breadth and depth of God's love although thousands of us have tried. Biblical writings, in themselves a form of beauty and doxology, emerge from within the human community's experience of the living God who speaks to us as both grace and love. Yet God's creative love is beyond all works of art and human imagination.

In creating, the loving God is like an artist creating a work of art that is full of harmony and surprise. Sun, moon and stars look down upon us daily, and too often we do not even notice them. Can you tell me what phase the moon is in this week? How many constellations can you name? Can you tell the difference between a planet and a star in the sky? These questions are not a quiz to determine your knowledge of astronomy. They are questions to lead you to reflect on your own powers of observation and imagination. Sometimes we do not see what surrounds us, and what we fail to see may be the incredible beauty of Creation and the magnificence of the Creator.

Christians and Jews attribute the work of Creation to God in their sacred writings. In the Genesis stories, which are the preeminent biblical writing on Creation, the authors attribute the work of Creation to God. In other biblical writings, both the Word and the Spirit are described as Creators. But the biblical writings recognise Creation principally as the work of the Father.

In the Genesis Creation story, God is both a power and a poet, for it is through the poetic word that God creates. The Book of Genesis states, "Then God said, 'Let there be light,' and light was made" (Gn. 1:3). The Genesis narrative of Creation demonstrates the power of God's word, as the authors have God speak simply, saying, "Let there be light, and there was light" (Gn. 1:3). God's Word is full of power. Creating is God's loving work of art.

The biblical story of Creation is not static. What

God brought into being in creating was the beginning of creating. God was Love before the beginning began, and God continues loving, creating, and nourishing as Creation continues. Creating is a continuing dynamic reality, always moving toward a new fullness.

The Creation story in Genesis is not a scientific exposition about how the cosmos came to be. This narrative tells us that it is God who brought the cosmos into being and that humankind is responsible for maintaining and protecting it. The Genesis narrative describes everything as being related from the beginning because it all begins with God. All forms of Creation need one another in some unique way, and all bear the imprint of their relationship with the divine Creator. The essence of God expresses itself in a relationship of tender and creative love with all that is. Creation is the work of God the Lover. All that is, is connected.

The Genesis story became part of the Jewish sacred Scriptures because the Israelites and Jews deliberately accepted these stories as explaining their experiences with reality. The Christian Church accepted these writings as Sacred Scriptures and professed that the Hebrew Scriptures express, reflect, and interpret the experience of the Church.

There are differences and likenesses between religious and scientific narratives. They are different forms of writing, and they emerge from different forms of research. Their sources are different, but they are not in conflict.

They appeal to different forms of experience – the scientific and the spiritual.

In the biblical book of Genesis, the authors begin the narrative of Creation with the words, "In the beginning when God created the Heavens and the Earth," and then proceed to describe how God creates. The narrative they wrote over time was accepted as an honest and truthful interpretation of "the beginning". The narrative was in harmony with the community's religious experience.

Scientists begin their investigation or study of Creation with a different yet somewhat similar process. They base their conclusions on observation, study, research, methodological interpretation, and previous scientific history. Finally, scientific theories must be shared with other scientists and scientific communities, and the acceptance or rejection of the theories depends on the conclusions of the scientific community.

One needs to read both the scientific and religious narratives from a particular perspective. A religious narrative arises out of a serious and prolonged process of deliberation within a religious community. The deliberation focuses on the nature of their religious experience with the world in which they lived. This Genesis narrative arises out of a people's commitment to God. The Genesis story is not a scientific exposition of the beginning. Unfortunately, some Christians believe the Genesis story is a scientific narrative. Biblical Creation stories are religious narratives, reflecting spiritual values, not scientific ones.

A story of deep delight emerges from Genesis (1:1 - 2:3). This biblical story begins with the words, "In the beginning," and tells us that in the beginning there was only a formless void and darkness. In the midst of this formless void, "a wind from God swept over the face of the waters". Then God began to speak, and with God's word Creation began.

This is a stunning narrative. In thirty-four short biblical verses, the author(s) wrote in poetic form a story about the Origin of all that is, about the beauty and goodness not only of Creation but also of the Creator. "In the beginning" God created all that is. The rhythm of the story is joyful, alive, bursting with energy. As God brings all things into being, the cosmos, the Earth, the waters, the sun, the rocks, the animals, the plants, and finally humankind, God rejoices, seeing that all of Creation is good. The authors indicate that whatever God creates, because it emerges from the love that is God, is "good". Among all creatures in the Book of Genesis, it is only humankind who is "very good," for God created humankind in the "image and likeness of God".

In singling out humankind, the authors of Genesis tell their readers or listeners that God intends human beings to be images of the divinity itself. God created human beings to be like God, living in a loving relationship with all that is. As God is creative, so humans are meant to be creative. As Trinity is diverse in a perfect communion of love, so humankind is meant to be a diverse community of love. As God lives passionately, so humankind is meant to live passionately. As God is alive in love, so every human person is called to be alive in love.

The authors of Genesis say these things about God because they interpreted their experiences of God in these ways. The authors saw patterns of mercy, goodness, and peace in their relationship with God. They also experienced rejection, cruelty, abuse, and disdain from not only their enemies but from one another. The people experienced both the goodness of God and their own goodness, and they also experienced their own selfishness and human inadequacy. In their lives the people knew that they often missed the mark of what they were called to be. They were never as holy and just and loving as God. They knew this and so they described their own experience as being both grace-filled and sinful.

The Genesis Creation story describes an Israelite understanding of God as Creator. It is a *theological* love story. It is both a personal and a communal love story, reflecting the religious faith of a community and the community's relationship with God over time. The Creation story is a narrative that called forth certain values and priorities from the Israelite community. For centuries the Israelites kept the story of Creation alive as one of their sacred stories. Eventually they accepted it as the beginning narrative of their Sacred Scriptures. In continuity, Christians recognised and accepted it as the story of their own beginning.

This Creation story is a song of wonder, of awe, of love, of response. It is full of heart. It is a love song, not unlike all love songs, reflecting not only the heart but also the intellect and the imagination of the authors. The Genesis story of Creation resounds with a brilliance that describes an incredible and startling intimacy between God and all of Creation.

Genesis begins by describing the emptiness or chaos before the beginning. Earth was "a formless void, with darkness in the midst of the deep," wrote the author. Almost parenthetically, the author reminds the reader that God is the Creator of all that is. Before God created, there was only God. In the beginning, the Earth was a formless void. Emptiness was the chaos from which God lovingly brought forth all that is.

Into the void came a wind, not just any wind, but "a wind from God". Christians suggest that this wind may refer to the Spirit who came upon the Christian community on Pentecost as "a strong wind". Christians relate the initial Creation to the beginning of the Church, when the Holy Spirit came upon the community. The life-giving and loving Spirit swept over the face of the Earth and everything was newly born.

The Creation story is not a fanciful story of what God is like. It is neither fiction nor science. It is the story of the God the Israelites experienced from the beginning, a beginning that moved into another new beginning with Abraham and Sarah and their family. It becomes the story of Moses leading the Israelites across the desert to Sinai and the story of their covenant with God. It is the story of the Israelites' entrance into the "promised land", and the beginning of a new nation. New beginnings offer a realisation of the experience of ever-new forms of relationship with God. Every new beginning is related. Creation is a continuing reality.

Whatever Christian people tell you about Creation, they tell you about the Father. This religious epic in Genesis, chapters one through eleven, gives life and meaning to the Judeo-Christian tradition, for it is the communal story of both Jews and Christians. It interprets important experiences of the Israelite-Jewish community over the centuries until the Incarnation of Jesus. It names special places and people, particular heroes, heroines, and even enemies and villains. It praises goodness and does not hide the people's sins. It looks forward to their future through the lens of their past.

The biblical story of Creation puts in perspective those past experiences which were life giving as well as those experiences that divided the people from one another and from God. This story and other biblical stories enabled the Israelites and Jews to make sense of their relationship with God, with one another, and with all of Creation. The Genesis writers saw that all of Creation was good, a gift from God. They wrote about the goodness of Creation from their observations and the minimal science that was known in their time and culture.

It is impossible to tell a love story without exaggeration. In love stories exaggeration tells the truth, and it is truth the authors are telling in Genesis. Whatever they knew or did not know about science, they recognised Creation as a gift from God, a gift that was good. The Book of Genesis describes God in myriad ways. God is creator, almighty, cosmic, judge, forgiver, lover. The narrative is a faith proclamation, not in the sense of a blind acceptance of inexplicable ideas, but a poetical and epical statement from a committed people about the nature of the God who brought and continues to bring love into being through Creation.

The Genesis story of Creation is a story by unknown authors who explain an unverifiable truth in a veiled way. No human being could have been present at the beginning of Creation, so the author or authors looked back from what they did know, to describe what they believed happened. They used a mythical timeline, "In the beginning", to tell how God initiated the Creation of all that is. The story ends by telling its readers, or listeners, that "God blessed the seventh day and hallowed it," because on it God rested from all the work of Creation.

From the beginning to the end of this story, the author extols the God who brought and continues to bring all of Creation into being. The author acknowledges that it is by God's powerful and loving word that God creates all that is. Within the Creation story each step of Creation ends with the refrain, "And God saw that it was good". That phrase refers not only to God's relationship with Creation but expresses how all of Creation is related through its goodness and through God as its creator.

Trinitarian Triads

At different times in Christian history, mystics, scholars, and Church leaders have suggested new triads for the persons of the Trinity. The traditional images of the Trinitarian triad given to us by Jesus are "the Father, the Son, and the Holy Spirit". If new images are to be used, they need to be faithful to the original triad, each image indicating both an intimate relationship among the Trinity and the unique differences of each person. The three images together should give a portrait of Trinitarian unity.

Many newer suggestions have been developed, but few have yielded theologically strong enough triads to speak of the oneness of Trinity. The primary need is for images that speak clearly about the diversity of each person and at the same time of the intimacy of the love relationship that unites them. New images faithful to the original biblical triad need to be conceived. Each suggestion of a new triad may offer some fresh insight about God, yet because of the nature of God and the nature of language, each triad does not always have the same value in naming God.

In the 20th Century, Karl Rahner, S.J., a preeminent theologian, described the persons of the Trinity: the Father is "the unoriginate Origin who is source of all;" the Son is "the Word self-expressed in history;" and the Spirit is "the uniting Love given and received". Rahner's images

and language initiated other attempts to name the persons
of the Triune God in an inclusive and mystical way. The
following are a few among proposed triads for Trinity:

SOURCE	FATHER	SON	SPIRIT
Bible	The Father	The Son	The Holy Spirit
Augustine	The Lover	The Beloved	Love
Hildegard of Bingen	A brightness	A flashing forth	A fire
Karl Barth	The Revealer	The Revelation	The Revealedness
Walter Kasper	A giver	A giver and receiver	A receiver
Karl Rahner	The unoriginate Origin	The Word self-expressed	The uniting Love
Elizabeth Johnson	Wisdom	Her beloved child	The Spirit of their mutual love
Sally McFague	Mother	Lover	Friend of the world that is God's body
Herbert Mulhen	I	Thou	We

The classic triad of God as Father, Son, and Holy
Spirit is the preeminent and traditional way in which the
Church names the persons of the Trinity, but sometimes
we need to jar ourselves with unexpected new metaphors
and images that encourage us to expand and deepen our
relationship with Trinity.

The Trinitarian Triad of St Augustine

In the 5th Century, St Augustine wrote a treatise on the Trinity in which he named the Trinitarian triad "the Lover," "the Beloved", and "Love" [*Amans, amatus, amor*]. This triad is particularly compelling because each of the images is dynamically alive and intimately related. The triad aligns itself with the traditional images, Father, Son, and Holy Spirit. To think of Trinity as the Lover, the Beloved, and Love is to see the Trinity in a new way. The One who is by nature indivisibly one in love is also three differentiated persons. Augustine's images are gender free, so Trinity remains pure spirit and at the same time is vibrantly alive. The Lover, Beloved, and Love image a dynamic community of love.

To speak of the "Lover" is to speak of the originator, the initiator, and the begetter. To speak of the "Beloved" is to speak of the begotten one, intimately related as a Son to his Father. To speak of the "Love" is to establish the character of the union of the three. To speak of the Lover, the Beloved, and the Love is to speak of Trinity's passionate and creative relationship of oneness in love.

Love is always alive, reaching out with goodness and peace. Perhaps the primary reason why Christians do not seem to respond to the Holy Spirit with the same love as with the Father or the Son is because the human images of a father and a son are part of human experience. On the other hand we all know what a Lover, a Beloved, and Love are. Because the model Augustine developed seems to be closer to the reality of the Trinity, I will begin to introduce Augustine's images in this book.

Augustine offered a new way to name the persons of the Trinity in the 5th Century after Christ. In the 12th Century, Hildegard of Bingen referred to the Trinity as "a brightness, a flashing forth, and a fire". Hildegard presented the Spirit as "Fire," undoubtedly remembering the "tongues of fire" that descended on all with the coming of the Holy Spirit. Both Augustine and Hildegard preserved the equality of the three persons and their differentiation, as well as their shared common life

Who is the God we Love? The Sermon on the Mount

The question, "Who is God?" is not simply a question of naming God as "Triune" or as "Father, Son, and Holy Spirit." It is a question about who God is and how God relates to humankind and all of Creation. "What is God really like?" people ask. And when someone replies, "God is three persons in one glorious relationship of love," the questioner often pauses and perhaps asks another question: "How can three persons be one God?" When we say, "the essence of God is relationship," other questions arise, such as, "How are we related to God?" and "What difference does such a relationship make in our lives?"

It is Jesus' response to these questions that gives insight into the nature of our relationship with God. In commissioning the disciples to go and preach the Gospel,

Jesus directs them to do so in the name of "the Father, the Son, and the Holy Spirit." Again and again in his preaching, Jesus told his followers and us something new about Trinity or something new about himself and his relationship with God. Jesus saw God as his Father. He saw himself as God's Son. The Sermon on the Mount is, in one sense, a sermon about morality and values, but it also a sermon on the love of Jesus for the Father and the Father's love for him and for us.

As we begin our reflection on the Sermon, let us remember that "mystery" does not refer simply to something we cannot understand, but to a truth that we can always understand more fully. Mystery is not simply an intellectual puzzle; we do not take hold of it through study. If we empty ourselves and rest in Trinity, the Mystery may take hold of us. When Trinity embraces us and we welcome that embrace, Trinity will take hold of us, enter into and alter us, and enlarge our perception of reality. The way in which we relate to Mystery can be transforming. When Mystery embraces us we may not even realise it, for sometimes it is difficult to accept our own loveliness.

Let us acknowledge for a moment that we know God as the Father or Lover through Jesus. If we want to know more about the Lover or Father, there is no person or place that can give us more insight than the Church– that is, the community of believers to whom we are joined by our faith commitment. The Scriptures are a privileged source for insight into our relationship with God because they share with us the word of God. When Jesus speaks about the Father or the Spirit in his sermons, he is telling us about his intimate relationship with God. In the Scriptures, Jesus speaks about his life, his experiences, his love, his laments, his friends, himself. There are few sources that will give us fuller insights into the Lover than Jesus' own words in the Gospels, and his sermons always have references to the Father. However, it is in *The Sermon on the Mount* that Jesus speaks most fully about the Father/Lover.

The Sermon on the Mount is a unique biblical treasure of teachings and short sayings of Jesus. Biblical sermons are not verbatim records of what Jesus said on a single occasion. Each one is a compilation of Jesus' sayings and teachings presented within a Gospel. Luke presents an abbreviated form of Matthew's *Sermon on the Mount* in chapter six of his Gospel.

The love and moral guidance of God the Father is a prominent theme in this sermon. It offers a pastoral image of God the Father that suggests how the Father / Lover loves and relates to humans and all of Creation. It directs us specifically on how to live in response to God's love. This sermon is filled with memorable phrases like "love your enemies" and "pray for those who persecute you" or "you cannot serve God and mammon". The phrases sound familiar for they are imbedded in our Christian heritage. Even after twenty centuries, they speak Jesus' message to us and continue to stir our listening hearts.

For just a moment imagine yourself seated on the grass, listening to someone tell you a story. The storyteller may be well known or someone you met just this morning. This person speaks to you and your family and friends kindly, gently. *The Sermon on the Mount* begins with Jesus preaching the eight beatitudes, blessings for those who live in any form of distress.

Jesus is explicit in naming the blessed, saying that blessed are the poor in spirit, those who mourn, those who are meek, the ones who hunger and thirst for righteousness. Jesus includes those who give mercy, as well as the pure in heart and the peacemakers. The qualities Jesus names in the blessings reflect the Father's love. God loves everyone who is suffering in any way and everyone who tries to relieve human suffering.

The people to whom Jesus spoke were poor and, in all likelihood, uneducated ordinary folk. Jesus' listeners were neither powerful people nor religious leaders. They included hardworking fishermen or tradespeople, people unseen by the privileged, maybe a bit rough-edged, people who might be described as "the hidden ones" or "the unnoticed". Jesus calls them all to himself. He would be their servant; they would be his friends.

Jesus speaks with conviction, commitment, and love. "You are the salt of the Earth," he says. "You are the light of the world." You hear the words congratulating you. You also hear them challenging you to "be perfect, therefore, as your heavenly Lover is perfect" (Matthew 5:48).

How does one live "perfectly? The Sermon on the Mount tells us:

> *You have heard that it was said, "An eye for an eye and a tooth for a tooth." But I say to you, do not resist an evildoer. But if anyone strikes you on the right cheek, turn the other also; and if anyone wants to sue you and take your coat, give your cloak as well; and if anyone forces you to go one mile, go also the second mile. Give to everyone who begs from you, and do not refuse anyone who wants to borrow from you.*
>
> Matthew – 5: 38-42

Jesus challenges his listeners to love everyone. He makes it clear that we are to be forgiving people, and that our Lover God "makes the sun rise on the Evil and on the Good, and sends rain on the righteous and on the unrighteous." "It is easy to love those who love you," says Jesus. He also challenges his listeners to change the way they relate to others. To some listeners, and perhaps to you and me, this seems a difficult and perhaps unreasonable expectation. But it is what our Lover God asks of us.

When we recognise how God expects us to relate to others, we may come to a new recognition of what it means to live a Christian life. The heavenly Lover models perfection and challenges us to follow the divine model. We need to love our enemies and ignore whatever abuse we experience. Our Lover expects us to love everyone.

The ethical challenges in this sermon are demanding. They ask for more than many of us think is possible to give. Jesus knows this. Matthew tells us that Jesus told them why they should live as he challenged them to do:

> *But I say to you, love your enemies and pray for those who persecute you, so that you may be children of our (Father-Lover) in Heaven; for our Lover makes the sun rise on the Evil and on the Good, and sends rain on the righteous and on the unrighteous.* – Mt. 5: 44-45

Jesus tells us to "do what our Lover says".

> *You have heard that it was said to those of ancient times, 'You shall not murder' and 'whoever murders shall be liable to judgment'. But I say to you that if you are angry with a brother or sister, you will be liable to judgment; and if you insult a brother or sister, you will be liable to the council; and if you say, 'You fool,' you will be liable to the hell of fire. So when you are offering your gift at the altar, if you remember that your brother or sister has something against you, leave your gift there before the altar and go; first be reconciled to your brother or sister, and then come and offer your gift (...) And if your right hand causes you to sin, cut it off and throw it away; it is better for you to lose one of your members than for your whole body to go into Hell.* – Mt. 5: 21-30

These recommendations address specific moral concerns. They begin with the basic Christian challenge to "Love your neighbour as yourselves".

Jesus called his listeners not only to love their friends but also to love their enemies. The word "enemies" indicates a harsh separation or rejection. An enemy is by definition one with whom you do not share a relationship of love. Enemies ordinarily share only bitterness. But when you love, you may "rejoice and be glad, for your reward is great in Heaven, for in the same way they persecuted the prophets who were before you" (5:12). When Jesus preached about how we should live, he refers us to our Lover who is in Heaven, who sees in secret, who will reward us.

Jesus preached a particular kind of response in many situations of conflict. "Do not store up for yourselves treasures on Earth, where moth and rust consume and where thieves break through and steal... rather store up for yourselves treasures in Heaven, where neither moth not rust consumes and where thieves do not break in and steal. For where your treasure is, there your heart will be also." It is clear what the foundation for morality is. It is love of Trinity and love of neighbour.

At the end of Matthew's Chapter Five, Jesus mentions the Lover for the first time. He describes the Lover as the perfect one who sees us as both salt and light. The Lover is the one to whom everyone should give glory. Glory is beyond all normal praise. "Glory" is absolute praise given only to Trinity. Those who give glory know they are unworthy of glory themselves, but there is a joy in being able to truly glorify Trinity. Giving glory is a way of giving praise to one who is beyond all praise. It is an offering of respect, love, even reverence to the astonishing and ever surprising Trinity who is our Lover, our Beloved, and the Love that makes us one.

This sermon of Jesus focuses on God the Lover whom Jesus described as not only being perfect, but as a model for human perfection. Jesus encouraged his followers to "be perfect as your heavenly Lover is perfect". Through his own daily life, through his words and deeds Jesus revealed the nature and character of our Lover in Heaven. It was not through words only but through his daily life, including sharing stories about his parents, his Jewish heritage, his friendship with the beloved disciples, with Martha, Mary, Lazarus, and with Mary Magdalene that Jesus reveals the nature of the Lover. We know the Lover through knowing Jesus. We love the Lover by sharing in Jesus' love of this same Lover.

The theme of "fatherhood" appears frequently throughout this sermon. Jesus uses the title "Father" repeatedly. Jesus modifies the title "Father" with the words "your" Father or "our" Father or "my" Father, or "our heavenly Father," indicating an intimate relationship between the Father and humankind. Jesus not only introduced "Father" as the principal image of God, but he used the word *Abba* (an intimate word) to indicate the kind of Father God is. For Jesus, "Father" or *Abba* was a title of affection that described a tender, strong, and loving relationship. It is no exaggeration to say that this sermon could also be called "The Sermon about the Loving Father". Jesus told his followers of the Father's providential love when he said:

> *Do not worry about your life, what you will eat or what you will drink; or about your body what you will wear. Is not life more than food, and the body more than clothing? Look at the birds of the air; they neither sow nor reap nor gather into barns, and yet your heavenly Lover feeds them. Are you not of more value than they?*
>
> – Mt. 6:25-26

The Lover provides an ecstatic, compassionate, providential love for humankind and all created reality. All of Creation and all of humankind reflect the wonder and passionate love of our Lover. All that is, is related to the Lover, the one who makes the sun rise and sends the rain on both the Evil and the Good. Our Lover loves both the righteous and the unrighteous. Jesus tells us that we are to live and love as the Lover lives and loves. We are to aim for perfection.

According to Jesus, when we pray we should do so in secret, not to receive compliments from our neighbours but to please our Lover, "and our Lover who sees in secret will reward us". When we give alms, we should beware of practicing piety before others. When fasting we should not "look dismal," but we should put oil on our head and wash our face so that our fasting may not be seen by others but by our Lover in Heaven, "who sees in secret and will reward you" (Mt. 6:16-18).

Throughout the *Sermon on the Mount*, Jesus calls all people to pray together, "Our Father/Lover who art in Heaven". God is the Lover of all. God is the Creator of the cosmos and all that the cosmos holds. Trinity is the Creator and all Creation is embedded in some way in God's Kingdom of Love. As God the Lover is one in love with the Beloved, and the Love that unites, so we are one in love with humankind, with all Creation, and with Trinity – the Lover, the Beloved, and the Love. Once Jesus' listeners recognise that God is the Lover of all, and that all of humankind are God's children, Jesus calls his listeners, including us, to relate in mutual love with both Trinity and one another. It is love that unites us with everything that is. Everything is connected because Trinity is love. Trinity calls all people to love one another and to care for all of natural Creation, which is Trinity's gift to us. We cannot live without one another. The gifts of Creation cannot live without our care for and protection of nature. The cosmos needs our loving care as much as we need its produce and beauty.

Jesus urged us to be one in love with God our Lover,

and with all that Trinity has made. It is through the Lover's passionate and fertile love that everything comes to be and is related. The cosmos and all who relate to it lovingly live a Trinitarian life. Everything that is, is related to Trinity, to God the Lover, to the Beloved, and to the Love that unites. The love to which Trinity calls us is not ordinary, for we are made in Trinity's image. Our love, like Trinity's love, is meant to be alive, steadfast, passionate, ecstatic, fertile, and relational. The words of Jesus' *Sermon on the Mount* lead us, as God's beloveds, into a world of connections and relationships – with the Father / Lover, the Son / Beloved, and the Spirit / Love.

THREE

THE MYSTERY OF THE BELOVED SON

Who do you say that I am?

In the Gospels, there are several occasions when Jesus speaks privately with his apostles. On one of those occasions Jesus asked the apostles about the meaning of a title applied to him: "Who do people say that the Son of Man is?" Jesus asked. The disciples responded by telling Jesus that people thought he was John the Baptist, or Elijah, or Jeremiah, or one of the prophets (Mt. 16:14). Then Jesus asked the really difficult question, "But who do you say that I am?" (Mk 8:29).

The disciples were silent, but as might be expected, their leader, the impetuous Peter, spoke out, saying: "You are the Messiah, the Son of the living God!" (Mt. 16:16). Jesus responded, "Blessed are you, Simon, son of Jonah! For flesh and blood has not revealed this to you, but my Father who is in Heaven" (Mt. 16:17). Jesus accepted this title, and at this point he blessed Peter for naming him "Messiah".

How do Christians of the 21st Century identify Jesus? What is your answer to his question, "Who do you say that I am?" Today Christians ordinarily name Jesus "the Lord", or "our Redeemer", and recognise Jesus as "the Saviour of the world". These and other titles speak for us, expressing our reason for being followers of Jesus. The titles we use for any person inform others of the nature of our relationship with that person. This chapter is a reflection on titles, like *Messiah*, which were used by some 1st Century Christians to name Jesus.

Religious groups ordinarily use images or titles to describe their leaders and the God whom they worship. However, Jewish worshippers do not so much as speak the name of God whom they profess to be beyond and above all names. Christians, on the other hand, profess that God relates to us. Jesus used the words "the Father", "the Son" and "the Holy Spirit" to introduce us to "Trinity". These titles are relational by nature. They tell us something about the relationship within Trinity. We describe our God in our prayer or through our hymns when we name God as "a mighty fortress", or "most holy Trinity". Christians use a variety of images for Jesus in the sacred Scriptures and in hymns. Christ is our "shepherd", or "the lamb of God". Multiple images reflect a multi-faceted God; every single title is inadequate by itself.

Many images or titles used to name God or Christ appear in hymns and prayers. Originally, most titles appeared in the Scriptures, especially in the psalms and Gospels. Some images have disappeared from hymns because they no longer seem to be adequate images of God or because they do not seem culturally appropriate. Following the renewal of the Second Vatican Council and the leadership of Pope Francis, Catholics today sing more often of the mercy and love of God than of warrior or power images.

The Image of Messiah

"Messiah" is only one of many titles given to Jesus in New Testament writings, but it is a primary image. The Hebrew word *mashiah* translates into the Greek word *Christos,* which translates into the Latin word *Christus,* which translates into the English word *Christ.* The word "Christ" is sometimes mistakenly thought to be a family name for Jesus. It is, in fact, a most significant title that Jesus used to identify himself, and it tells us who some of the first Christians thought Jesus was. In Israelite and Jewish history, *Messiah* was a title preserved for the one who would be the ideal leader of the Israelites. The Jews believed God would send them a messiah to lead Israel to national greatness.

The Hebrew title *Messiah* pointed to "the anointed one" as the one chosen by God. Because the Israelites thought their ideal ruler would be a king, they asked the Judge, Samuel, to find a king "to govern us". Samuel prayed to the Lord and the Lord said to Samuel, "Listen to their voice and set a king over them" (1Sm. 8:22). Samuel chose Saul to be the first Israelite king. He took a vial of oil and poured it on Saul's head and kissed him, saying, "The Lord has anointed you to rule over his people Israel. You shall reign over the people of the Lord and you will save them from the hand of their enemies all around them." (1Sm. 10:1)

No one could anoint himself. It was God who chose the "anointed one". From the beginning of the Christian Church, those who chose Jesus as their Lord were anointed with oil at their Baptism. This anointing was a sign of their relationship with the Christ, the Risen Lord.

"Christ" is the English 'equivalent' of "Messiah". The title "Christ" recognises and affirms that Jesus is the one sent from God, the ideal leader, the anointed one. Jesus, risen and glorified, is "the Christ". His followers were, like him, God's anointed ones. "Jesus" is the first name of the human son of Mary. In his humanity, the "Word made flesh", the Son of God, is Jesus. After his death-resurrection-glorification, his followers named him "the Christ", the anointed one. Both Jewish and Gentile Christians recognised Jesus as the "Messiah" for whom the Jews waited.

Today Christians do not ordinarily name Jesus "the Messiah". In modern times, the word "Messiah" carries connotations of an ideal earthly ruler, a king like other kings. Jesus, the Christ, was not an earthly leader, nor was he in the ordinary sense a "king". However, during the Advent season when Christians gather to celebrate the birth of Christ, they sing George Frederic Handel's oratorio *Messiah*. Communities of singers, musicians, families, and churches praise the birth and identity of "the Messiah", that is, the Christ. Often, when the great *Halleluiah* chorus begins, the conductor will turn to the audience and invite the people to sing the chorus with the choir. The music and the text together make this a solemn, faith-filled moment for those Christians who sing *Messiah* even twenty-one centuries after Peter's declaration.

How were the title *Messiah* and other titles for Jesus preserved and handed on to Christians in the decades after Jesus death-resurrection? First, they were handed on through the preaching of the apostles and disciples. The written texts of the New Testament, especially the Gospels, tell us that the community proclaimed Jesus "the Christ" shortly after his death-resurrection. Later, other titles were added through preaching and church prayers, including hymns.

Lex Orandi, Lex Credendi

Lex Orandi, Lex Credendi is an ancient principle that describes how Christian prayer and beliefs relate to one another. The way we pray is the way we profess our faith commitment and articulate why we are disciples of Jesus. Geoffrey Wainwright interprets this principle to mean that "what is prayed indicates what may and must be believed". This old Latin adage is a succinct way to state how our prayer and our beliefs relate. Wainwright explains the *orandi/credendi* principle by saying that worship influences doctrine and doctrine influences worship. Ordinarily worship precedes the formulation of doctrine.

When Christians gather to sing *Messiah* today they are praying, and as they pray to and about the Christ (Messiah) they sing what they believe, understand, and commit themselves to. It is for this reason that any early hymn texts that are available to us today are significant. The texts tell us in whom the 1st Century Church believed. It is surprising in some ways to recognise the relationship between 1st Century images of Christ and new images we are meeting in evolutionary-conscious theology.

The Christological Hymns

There are in the New Testament approximately thirty poetic passages that are the texts of hymns sung by 1st Century Christian churches. The hymn texts were not always written by the New Testament author of the document in which they appear. Most often the hymn texts were composed for community prayer and at a later date inserted in New Testament texts by Paul and other New Testament authors.

Seven of these hymn texts are Christological, that is, they use images and descriptions to name the risen and glorified Christ. In all probability, the author of each epistle heard Christian communities sing these texts as prayer and simply wanted to share them with the communities to whom they wrote. None of the original melodies of the hymns have been preserved in the Scriptures, though new melodies for the older hymns are still being composed.

Some of the best-known hymns in the New Testament are in the Gospel of Luke: the angels' *Gloria in excelsis Deo* (2:14), Simeon's *Nunc Dimittis* (2:29-32), Zechariah's *Benedictus* (1:68-79), and Mary's *Magnificat* (1:46-55). The hymn that introduces the Gospel of John, *The Prologue* (1:1-18) is a sublime poem that one scholar described as too beautiful to be written by the hand of a human person.

The two hymns we will examine in this chapter are one in the Epistle to the Philippians (2:5-11) possibly written between 54 and 57 CE, and the second in the epistle to the Colossians (1:15-20), probably written by a disciple of Paul as late as 80-100 CE. These two hymns are longer than most hymn texts and scholars indicate that they present the thinking of Christians possibly as early as 49 CE.

These hymn passages share a common form. They are poetic, using images and having an obvious rhythm. Some hymns are like lyrical love letters, each one expressing a deep relationship with the Christ, the loving Word of God who is sometimes described in cosmic ways. We do not know the date of their composition. We do know that they preceded the date of the epistles in which they were included.

The dates when the epistles were written are significant because an earlier date, like that of the Philippians, the decade of the 50s CE, represents the thinking of Christian communities formed shortly after the death-resurrection of Jesus. Although there is not full agreement on the date of Colossians, the later date of Colossians, possibly in the 70s CE, indicates what Christians were thinking in the latter quarter of the century. It is apparent that images used in mid-1st Century were also used thirty to fifty years later. Interestingly, even today Christians sing some of these hymns. What we pray is what we believe.

The Christological Hymn in Philippians, 2:5-11

This epistle begins with a greeting from Paul and Timothy to the church of Philippi, a small town in the Roman province of Macedonia. It was written while Paul was in prison, in or about 49 CE. Paul knew the people of the church of Philippi well. His introduction is friendly as he thanks "my God every time I remember you, constantly praying with joy in every one of my prayers for all of you" (Ph. 1:3).

Paul writes to the Philippians with affection. His first paragraphs are loving and harmonious. They indicate that Paul has a special relationship with this church, possibly because this was the first church Paul planted in Europe. Paul gives praise for all that God has done for the Philippians. His words are full of life and a joyous spirit runs through the epistle. The heart of Paul speaks as he thanks the church for "sharing in the Gospel," and he lets the Philippians know that he prays for all of them.

Early in this letter Paul inserted what is now one of the most revered of Christian hymns (2:5-11).

THE MYSTERY OF THE BELOVED SON

Let the same mind be in you that was in Christ Jesus,
who, though he was in the form of God,
did not regard equality with God
as something to be exploited,
but emptied himself,
taking the form of a slave,
being born in human likeness.
And being found in human form,
he humbled himself
and became obedient to the point of death –
even death on a cross.

Therefore God also highly exalted him
and gave him the name
that is above every name,
so that at the name of Jesus
every knee should bend,
in Heaven and on Earth and
under the Earth,
and every tongue should confess
that Jesus Christ is Lord,
to the glory of God the Father.

This is a "Christological" hymn describing both the human Jesus and the glorified Christ. The early Church sought to make known not only the whole life of Jesus and his glorification, but also the nature of the God whom Jesus made present among his people. The hymn has two complementary parts. The beginning verses, five through eight, exhort the singers to be of one mind with "Christ Jesus" and to live as he did, emptying himself, being humble and being obedient even unto death. The second half of the hymn is a song of praise and honour for Jesus whom God "highly exalted". Verses nine through eleven praise Christ the Lord, who is "the glory of God the Father."

Be "of the same mind as Christ Jesus," the hymn requests. This stanza is clearly a reference to what would be called today "the cosmic Christ". Christ was no small figure. God gave Christ the name "that is above every name". At this name – Jesus – "every knee should bend, in Heaven, and on Earth and under the Earth (...) Jesus Christ is Lord, to the glory of God the Father."

The first stanza is directed to the local church. "Shape up!" it seems to be saying. For the one who "was in the form of God did not regard equality with God as something to be exploited". Be humble. Be a servant. Empty yourselves. There is not only a relationship between Christ and the Father, but also a strong love relationship to be built up among the community with Christ.

> *Let the same mind be in you that was in Christ Jesus,*
> *who, though he was in the form of God,*
> *did not regard equality with God*
> *as something to be exploited,*
> *but emptied himself,*
> *taking the form of a slave,*

being born in human likeness.
And being found in human form,
he humbled himself
and became obedient to the point of death –
even death on a cross.

This first half of the hymn describes "Christ Jesus" as "in the form of God". The congregation professes implicitly that Christ is one with God as the Beloved Son. He is the one whom John calls the "Word made flesh," the promised and hoped for one, who "did not regard equality with God as something to be exploited..." He was both equal with God and humble; he did not take advantage of his divinity.

Through this hymn, the congregation proclaims its desire to be like Jesus, to have the same disposition as Jesus, the Christ. The human life of Jesus is seen through the image of total self-giving for others. He who was above all, who was in the form of God, emptied himself, becoming a servant to all. The hymn states unequivocally in verse six that Jesus was not only like God but equal to God. The hymn is a prayer that God's people might be humble and exalted at the same time, as Jesus the Christ was humble and exalted. The words tell us that the singing congregation did not fear but rejoiced in the exaltation and humility of the Christ they loved so mightily.

The Philippian hymn text proclaims that God's love is beyond every expectation. At a later date Paul wrote to the Romans that while it was not unusual for a person to die for another "good" person, "it was while we were still sinners that Christ died for us" (Rm. 5: 8). The Philippian Church sang an exalted, glorious theology of God as love. We learn from this hymn that they experienced God's love as beyond all understanding. This hymn is a majestic proclamation of faith.

The second stanza of this hymn, verses 2:9-11, shifts from describing the human Jesus to exalting the Christ:

> *Therefore God also highly exalted him*
> *and gave him the name*
> *that is above every name,*
> *so that at the name of Jesus*
> *every knee should bend,*
> *in Heaven and on Earth and*
> *under the Earth,*
> *and every tongue should confess*
> *that Jesus Christ is Lord,*
> *to the glory of God the Father.*

Here the focus changes from the incarnation and the humility of Jesus to his divinity and his exaltation by God. These last three verses – nine, ten, and eleven – form just one short, glorious sentence. Christ is above all, beyond all, with all. Jesus is "the glory of the Father". Jesus is Lord. He is the Beloved Son of God. He is one with God. For him, every knee should bend "in Heaven and on Earth and under the Earth". All humanity should join God in

THE MYSTERY OF THE BELOVED SON

exalting Jesus. In this hymn it is not Christians who exalt Jesus. It is not even Paul or his disciples who exalt. It is God who exalts Jesus-God who "gave him the name that is above every name".

Using St Augustine's model of Trinity, we could say that it is God the Lover who exalts the Beloved through Love. Trinitarian life is implicit in this hymn. The Father, the Son, and the Spirit are the Lover, the Beloved, and the Love.

From the beginning of this hymn, the church of Philippians sang of God's exaltation of Jesus. The earliest Christians acknowledged this unique relationship of Father and Son, of Lover and Beloved. They recognised and sang of Jesus as the one glorified by God. Through their lives and their words ("every knee should bend in Heaven and on Earth and under the Earth") they worshipped him. From the beginning, Greek as well as Jewish Christians believed that the God of Jesus was a living and loving God.

Through the revelation of Jesus, not just his words but through the model of his life, the first Christians understood that Jesus' relationship to God was special and unique. This insight led them to make enormous changes in their perception of who they were and who God is. Once it was the Jews who recognised themselves as God's people. In his final commission to his Jewish apostles and disciples, Jesus urged them to "Go and baptise all nations". With those words, Jesus proclaimed that all people are God's people.

The first Christians recognised that there is no limit to God's love long before Augustine used language to name

Trinity the Lover, the Beloved, and the Love. There is no limit to the glory and praise we can give to God, for Heaven and Earth are all in the realm of God's glory. God lives as a communion of Love overflowing with compassion not only for the Jews but for all peoples of all times and nations. God's love is universal. God embraces all that exists with love. God embraces Creation. God exalts Jesus. The Triune God is relational. Everything and everyone is connected by love.

The second half of the Philippian hymn describes an exalted Christ who is above every name. It took time for people to absorb the wonder of God's universal love and it was not until one of the last written epistles, the first epistle of John, that a Christian author could actually write: "God is love" (Jn. 4:8). All who are, are God's beloveds; all that is, is God's beloved. God's love extends to all people and all of Creation.

The Christological hymn in Philippians proclaims the "cosmic" Christ through both the form and text of this hymn. It is poetry in form and exaltation in text. The Philippian church proclaims in hymnody that it is not they but God who exalts Jesus, so that "at the name of Jesus every knee should bend, in Heaven and on Earth and under the Earth, and every tongue should confess that Jesus Christ is Lord, to the glory of God the Father." The text lifts up and gives glory to those who sing it. This hymn is a confession of faith and a proclamation of love for the exalted Christ.

The Philippian hymn is one of the most beautiful of all Christian hymns. It is lyrical, registering not only the deep humility and thanksgiving of the community that sings it, but also the exaltation of the incarnate and risen Christ It glorifies the humble as well as the cosmic Christ. It calls everyone to live like Jesus. It is no wonder that Paul incorporated it into his letter to the Philippians. Twenty centuries after Jesus' death this hymn is still being sung by Christian communities.

The Christological Hymn in Colossians 1:15-20

The letter to the Colossians begins with a typical greeting identifying the author as, "1 Paul, an apostle of Christ Jesus by the will of God, and Timothy our brother." The author then addresses those to whom he is writing, "2 To the saints and faithful brothers and sisters in Christ in Colossae," and he greets them with the blessing, 3 Grace to you and peace from God our Father."

This letter is one of the later Pauline epistles written near the end of the 1st Century CE to the church in Colossae, an ancient site in the present country of Turkey. Some scholars believe it was written by a disciple of Paul, and that Paul was already dead. At the time of its writing, Colossae was populated by both Jews and Roman citizens. The author gives thanks for the faith and love of the community, and he prays that the Colossians may "be filled with the knowledge of God's will in all spiritual wisdom and understanding". The introduction to the epistle is formal and prayerful and in the first chapter, the author introduces a Christological hymn of great spirit and depth.

The Colossian hymn (1:5-11) is quite different from that of the Philippians although it relates to it as a Christological hymn. It is of profound significance for it sings with focus, clarity, and profundity of the glorified Christ. It differs from Philippians in that the cosmic Christ is the one who envelops the whole of Creation with love. Every line is a line of glorification.

He is the image of the invisible God, the first born of all Creation; for in him all things in Heaven and on Earth were created, things visible and invisible, whether thrones or dominions or rulers or powers –all things have been created through him and for him.

He himself is before all things, and in him all things hold together.

He is the head of the body, the church; he is the beginning, the firstborn from the dead, so that he might come to have first place in everything.

For in him all the fullness of God was pleased to dwell, and through him God was pleased to reconcile to himself all things,whether on Earth or in Heaven, by making peace through the blood of his cross.

In the first words the author of the hymn describes the Christ as "the image of the invisible God". He is "the firstborn of all Creation". One cosmic image follows another: in Christ, "all things in Heaven and on Earth were created, things visible and invisible." The poetic text focuses on the Word who existed before anything came to be, and on the glorified Christ through whom "God reconciled to himself all things, whether on Earth or in Heaven, by making peace through the blood of his cross."

This hymn proclaims universal images of the Christ, "the firstborn of all Creation," and "the firstborn from the dead". Christ's relationship to all reality is astounding. All that is relates to Christ, and the Christ includes all that is in universal love. This is the living and loving cosmic Christ whom the singers glorify. The community at Colossae sang of the Christ as "the fullness of God". The singers proclaim the Christ as one with God, with the Creator from the beginning, intimately One. The Christ in Colossians is, as Robert Karris says, "the universal Lord".

This is a song of worship. It was undoubtedly sung at communal prayer. It is strong, powerful poetry, resembling the Prologue of John's Gospel. In singing this hymn, the whole community, the Colossae Church, confessed its commitment to and worship of the Christ, the cosmic and universally beloved redeemer. This hymn is a song of the exaltation of opposites such as "nearness" and "distance" from Christ. It praises the glorified Christ and names Christ as the Word made Flesh, uniting him as one with the Father and the Spirit from whom the Word can never be separated.

I can almost hear the Colossians sing this hymn with full voice:

He is before all things, and in him all things hold together. He is the head of the body, the Church. He is the beginning, the firstborn from the dead. In him the fullness of God was pleased to dwell. Through him God was pleased to reconcile to himself all things, whether on Earth, or in Heaven, by making peace through the blood of his cross.

This is the cosmic Christ who is the reconciler and the peacemaker, as well as the first-born. It is an astonishing text that expresses the Christ's Trinitarian bond of love as well as his bond of love for the church of Colossae and all of Creation.

The Colossians looked from their small home on the Earth and saw through their imaginations the clouds and the distances leading to the above; and beyond all aboves, they looked to God. They saw through their hearts all that was between them and God. The universe made of "Heaven," the dome above, and the "Earth" below, and to the Creator, Word, and Spirit who brought all of the cosmos into life. The Triune God, bonded in intense, intimate, and immeasurable love, reaches out in love to all people, and the people of the Church of Colossae responded with this hymn.

If the hymn in Philippians was "low" Christology, the hymn in Colossians is surely "high" Christology. The imagination of the writer and of the worshippers stretched beyond Earth, beyond Nazareth, Jerusalem, and Israel, beyond the warrior nations that neighboured them, beyond what they could see or touch or even imagine. "He himself," they sang, "is before all things, and in him all things hold together." All things – wherever they may be. This was no small God to whom the Colossians spoke or whom they loved. "For in him all things in Heaven and on Earth were created, things visible and invisible, whether thrones or dominions or rulers or powers, all things have been created through him and for him."

This grand vision of God emerges from the Genesis story into the Church of Colossae. It recalls the God of Creation and the one who brought into being light and a dome in the sky to separate the sky from the waters, the day from the night. To lessen the darkness, this loving God separated the lesser light, the moon, so it may lighten the night. And whatever God created, "God saw that it was good". This is the same God who let the waters bring forth swarms of living creatures and birds and sea monsters and every living creature that moves and with which "the waters swarm, and every winged bird of every kind". Here is continuity and newness, and the continuity is in harmony with the Jewish tradition, while newness is Christ among universal Creation. The Christ is one with God and with everything that exists. "He himself is before all things, and in him all things hold together." The Christ holds the cosmos from the beginning, to now, and always.

This short hymn unabashedly worships the divine Christ. The community sings, "1 For in him all the fullness of God was pleased to dwell." What audacity and boldness!

What a resounding separation from the culture in which the Colossians themselves were immersed!

The final two lines celebrate the universality of Christ's love, for through his love "God was pleased to reconcile to himself all things, whether on Earth or in Heaven, by making peace through the blood of his cross." The scope of Christ's power is infinite. It is power for love and peace, for reconciliation and unity. The Colossians sang for that which was almost beyond hope, but they sang with the conviction of their faith.

In the text of this hymn the composer and the singers named Jesus the Christ, One with the Father, the Head of the Body the Church, the Beginning, the Firstborn from the Dead, God's Reconciler, Peacemaker and Redeemer. Scholars are not sure if Paul or a disciple of Paul or someone else wrote this epistle, but whoever wrote these words gave us a treasure. We have been given words that even after two thousand years continue to ring out with joy and nobility. The words bring hope to the downtrodden, relief to the weary, and peace to suffering human hearts.

The author of this hymn moves to outer space, to the realm of distant galaxies, without even knowing that the galaxies exist. The author moves beyond what is known of the universe to all that is unknown. With thankful hearts those who sang this hymn moved beyond the surface of life to give praise to Christ, to God, to the Spirit, to the unimaginable yet beautifully imagined cosmos. Those who prayed this hymn saw themselves living in a world far bigger than they, yet they were filled with hope, not fear, for they knew the cosmic Christ was with them among all of Creation.

Who is the God we Love?

The Latin epigram *Lex Orandi, Lex Credendi* states, "the law of prayer is the law of belief." As an epigram, it briefly states the relationship that exists between a community's prayer/worship and its belief/doctrine. *Lex Orandi, Lex Credendi* tells us that our experience of prayer as Church influences our beliefs as Church, and at the same time these beliefs influence how we pray as Church.

At the same time, whether we recognise it or not, our experience of being Church alters the way we pray and what we believe. Everything is related. Our daily experience of loving and being loved by and within the Church shapes and deepens our faith commitment. Our prayer, acts of justice, and the formation of Christian values direct our lives. It is not the formulas of our prayer or our formulas of beliefs that make us Church. All that we do and say, believe and love shape us as Church.

Our prayer, particularly our community prayer, is often transformative in our lives. Prayer may be life changing simply because when we pray from the mind and the heart together, and from a sustaining humility, we continue to grow spiritually. We are always in a state of becoming.

One of the more common prayer forms is hymnody. Hymns are a sung form of prayer, and the hymns we love may remain our favourites for decades. The hymns we love say what is in our hearts. We sing our love with our friends in faith, and repeating some hymns cause them to take hold of us, because they express our faith in an extraordinary way. In this chapter you examined two hymns written in the 1st Century as prayers for the Christian faith-community. These two hymns speak of Christ through metaphor. Remembering that the Philippian hymn and the Colossian hymn are both prayers, we asked, "What do these hymns tell us about the 1st Century Christian Church and its relationship with the Triune God that could lead us to a deeper love relationship between ourselves, our community, and Trinity?"

Pope Francis gives us a clue to early Christian beliefs in the first sentence of his encyclical *Laudato Si*. The Pope tells his readers that St Francis of Assisi reminded us that "our common home is like a sister with whom we share our life and a beautiful mother who opens her arms to embrace us." Pope Francis' encyclical is entitled "Our Care for Our Common Home," and that "common home" is the cosmos.

The cosmos is no small thing. It is the universe. The opposite of the cosmos is void or emptiness. The cosmos is not chaotic but harmonious. Its age is almost unimaginable, for scientists tell us that it is about 13.7 billion years old. It is large beyond our comprehension. Yet, the cosmos is our common home. Somehow the cosmos can seem too big for us. We have gotten comfortable on a small planet called Earth. We think we can handle Earth's magnitude, but the magnitude of the cosmos is unfathomable. How can we ever consider the cosmos our "home"?

Christians of the 1st Century used cosmic terms to describe the Risen Lord because they recognised and revered the Christ who was above all and beyond all. All things were created through him and for him (Col 1:16f), they sang. Their images of a cosmic Christ said, perhaps better than we in the 21st Century can say, that all that is comes from and is subject to the Christ. Christ, the Word, the Son,

is the image of the invisible God,
the firstborn of all Creation; (...)
He himself is before all things,
and in him all things hold together.
He is the head of the body, the church.

Why were cosmic titles and descriptions significant ways to name the Risen Christ in the 1st Century, and why were they uncommon Christological names in most of the following centuries? Are we just beginning in the 21st Century to return to the image of the Triune God as "cosmic"? If so, what does the adjective "cosmic" tell us about the Triune God?

Historically, theology is always infused with cultural themes. From the beginning, the Israelite people saw God as alive and active in their lives. God called Abraham and told him to "1 Go from your father's house to the land that

I will show you. I will make of you a great nation (...) 4 So Abraham went" (Gn. 1:1,4). The descendants of Abraham, Isaac, and Jacob believed that God related not only to individuals but to the whole people or tribe. Their God was cosmic even if they did not use the word "cosmic" or know the scientific meaning we apply to it today.

As the revelation of God, Jesus revealed a cosmic God. Jesus revealed that "God is love". God is the Creator of all that is. God is the Giver of Life, the Paschal Lamb, whose blood was shed for us, the prodigal Father, the Good Shepherd, the woman who searched for a lost coin. God is over and above and beyond all imaginable reality, yet God offers to be our servant and asks to be our friend.

Through his whole life, in his words and deeds, Jesus revealed God to be loving, healing, forgiving, and grace giving. In the first centuries after Jesus, his followers described the Risen Christ as God, not only with the language of love but also with the recognition that God was cosmic – above all, beyond all, close to all, within all. Jesus revealed, indirectly, through his person, that anthropomorphism was not an adequate or true way to describe God. God is not like us. God is exalted beyond all else and is to be praised and glorified as no one else can be. Yet we are created to be like God.

The mutual sharing of the Son and the Spirit in the Father's creative works includes not only bringing all that is into existence but also inviting all-that-is to accept the embrace of divine love. As God is cosmic, so Christ is cosmic. Trinity is cosmic, calling all people to embrace in cosmic love.

In the 1960s, when the exploration of space by humans began, ordinary people unfamiliar with basic scientific concepts began to realise how much they did not know about the universe in which they lived. Many people were startled and highly engaged by space discovery. Scientific knowledge was not only desirable but necessary in order to begin to understand the universe in which we live.

As one of those ordinary people with little scientific background, when I read the texts of the hymns in the letters to the Philippians or the Colossians, I am exhilarated and I ask myself, "How could the people of the 1st Century speak so readily and with wonder about the 'cosmic' Christ?" To speak of the cosmos is to speak of transcending magnitude. Cosmology looks at the whole and views the whole in relation to its parts. To describe the Christ as "cosmic" today is a welcome rediscovery. From the beginning, Christians recognised the Christ as the transcendent, living heart of all that is.

When I first read Saint Augustine's treatise on the Trinity, I was in awe of the way in which the 4th Century Church could be so personally and communally engaged with the Triune God. Augustine and Gregory of Nyssa both told us that the theology of Trinity was enthusiastically received in their day: "One could hardly walk through the market place without becoming engaged in a conversation about the Trinity." It seems that 4th Century Christians were far more engaged with the Triune God than were many Christians in the 20th Century. When and how did we lose our way?

Karl Rahner, S.J., wrote, "Christians are, in their practical life, almost mere 'monotheists.' We must be willing to admit that, should the doctrine of the Trinity have to be dropped as false, the major part of religious literature could well remain virtually unchanged." Somehow after the first millennium, the mystery of the Trinity ceased to dance or sing in the Church as it once did. Response to the Triune God no longer lifted up Christians or spurred them on. The Trinity became a philosophical puzzle; at its worst, it became an arithmetical puzzle, "How can three be one?" The question should have been "What does God being Trinity mean to us?"

As the heart of Trinity is universal cosmic love, so the Triune God relates to all that is through a love that is all-encompassing. Trinity embraces itself lovingly and moves out through its inner love to create and embrace with love all people and all that is. The first Christians recognised through the words of Jesus that God was triune – Father, Son, and Spirit, one in love within itself, and one in love with all that is.

The letters to the Philippians and the Colossians demonstrate that the Triune God relates intimately, passionately, and creatively with the people, but God's love is not a one-way love-fest. God loves us and asks for our love in return. Every aspect of our lives can relate to the harmony in Trinity's loving intimacy. These hymns of the Philippian and Colossian epistles are early records of the faith of these Christian communities, whether the members were culturally Jewish or Greek. Their hymns are a response to the question: "Who do you say that I am?" Those early Christians sang what they believed, and hymns sung from both the heart and the head brought new life, grace, conversion, and commitment to a nascent Church. When we sing these same hymns, from both the heart and the head, they can bring new life to our open hearts. *Lex orandi, lex credendi!*

Within the past half century, because of climate change and environmental concerns, our society is renewing and redeveloping its understanding of humankind's relationships to the natural world. Space-penetrating telescopes enable us to see beyond our stars and begin to realise the unimaginable scope of the universe. New discoveries of science lead us to recover the images of the cosmic Christ in our Scriptures and in the early Christian hymns:

> *Let the same mind be in you that was in Christ Jesus,*
> *who, though he was in the form of God,*
> *did not regard equality with God*
> *as something to be exploited,*
> *but emptied himself,*
> *taking the form of a slave,*
> *being born in human likeness.*
> *And being found in human form,*

he humbled himself
and became obedient to the point of death –
even death on a cross.
Therefore God also highly exalted him
and gave him the name
that is above every name,
so that at the name of Jesus
every knee should bend,
in Heaven and on Earth and
under the Earth,
and every tongue should confess
that Jesus Christ is Lord,
to the glory of God the Father.

FOUR

THE MYSTERY OF
SPIRIT-LOVE

The Breath of Love

> *Once upon a time there was Trinity, only Trinity.*
> *Before the beginning, before anything was,*
> *before everything was,*
> *Trinity was.*
> *Full of energy,*
> *Trinity embraced and generated new life.*
> *Trinity loved*
> *and everything began.*
> *Trinity, being the overflowing fullness of Love,*
> *brought forth new love*
> *and all that is came into being.*

Time began when Trinity began creating. The Lover-Father created new love by loving. The Beloved-Word spoke love harmoniously and eloquently. Spirit-Love danced and love moved lightly on the breath of God. Before the beginning Trinity lived in love, Trinity created and the beginning began. Trinity spoke, Trinity breathed--and new life and new love began to breathe with Trinity. A chorus of love began to sing praise and glory to Trinity as created beings continued to evolve and expand over and over again. Into our immeasurable future, the expanding universe will continue evolving and expanding and multiplying life and love, world without end. Amen.

The Coming of Spirit-Love

On Pentecost Sunday Christians celebrate the coming of the Holy Spirit to the followers of Jesus. There are two different passages in the New Testament that tell this story. One narrative is in John's Gospel, the other in Luke's *Acts of the Apostles*. Although John describes the coming of the Spirit in just two short verses, he depicts the disciples' frame of mind as well as their behaviour both before and after the coming of the Spirit. These insights give us an understanding of the ways in which the early faith community responded to the Pentecostal event.

The Gospel of John, Chapter 20:1-23, tells how on the day we now call "Easter," the followers of Jesus, both men and women, first learned of the empty tomb from Mary Magdalene. Mary went to Jesus' tomb early on Sunday to anoint the body of Jesus. She discovered the empty tomb, and brought this information to Jesus' followers who were already frightened. Their inability to resolve the problem of Jesus' missing body was the beginning of a sequence of events in which fear grew among the disciples. They were frightened on Sunday morning, but by the end of that day they were fearless, preaching publicly and fervently of the death-resurrection of Jesus. What happened between the morning and evening on that day? John tells us that,

> When it was evening on that day, the first day of the week, and the doors of the house where the disciples had met were locked for fear of the Jews, Jesus came and stood among them and said, "Peace be with you." After he said this, he showed them his hands and his side. Then the disciples rejoiced when they saw the Lord. Jesus said to them again, "Peace be with you. As the Father has sent me, so I send you." When he had said this, he breathed on them and said to them, "Receive the Holy Spirit. If you forgive the sins of any, they are forgiven them; if you retain the sins of any, they are retained."

Luke, in Acts, tells of the coming of the Spirit in a slightly different way. The disciples were gathered in the upper room on the Jewish Pentecost Day.

> Suddenly from Heaven there came a sound like the rush of a violent wind, and it filled the entire house where they were sitting. Divided tongues, as of fire, appeared among them, and a tongue rested on each of them. All of them were filled with the Holy Spirit and began to speak in other languages, as the Spirit gave them ability.
>
> – Acts 2: 2-5

Both John and Luke describe the followers of Jesus as gathered together in fear and prayer. In John's Gospel the risen Christ suddenly appears to them, breathes on them, and says, *"Receive the Holy Spirit."* In Luke's account they are hidden in a house for fear of the Jews, and suddenly, with the sound of a violent wind and the appearance of tongues of fire, the Spirit comes to them. Transformed by the Spirit's presence they lost their fear and went out to preach publicly. Through Jesus' act of breathing upon them and saying, "Receive the Holy Spirit," Christ gave new life to his friends. It is the Holy Spirit who gave the disciples the new energy and the fire of love that led them to preach the Mystery of Jesus' death-resurrection-glorification.

Jesus breathed and prayed over the disciples, giving them their mission. His gift takes two forms: first, in John, the act of breathing and the accompanying words, "Receive the Holy Spirit," and second, in Acts, the noise of the wind, the sight of the fire, and the gift of tongues. Jesus gave the disciples new life, the life of the Holy Spirit. He also informed the disciples that the Father had sent him, and he, by giving the Holy Spirit to them, was sending them just as the Father had sent him. In this conversation Jesus acknowledges the presence of both the Father and Spirit with him and with them. With the coming of the Holy Spirit, Trinity embraced the disciples with divine love.

The Holy Spirit is the spirit of life, of energy, and of love. In John's account, the Spirit sent by the Father through the

Word brought a new life of love not only to individuals but to the community of believers as a whole. The life and love of Trinity entered into the disciples through the Spirit in a new way, and they no longer hid in fear. They went forth deliberately, inspired by the Spirit to bring the good news of Jesus to the world.

Luke's story of the coming of the Holy Spirit is more detailed than John's. In both, Jesus appears to the "disciples." In Luke those present are the "disciples, women and men." In both John and Acts, they are all hiding "for fear of the Jews." In John, Jesus "breathed" on them. In Acts, the sound "like the rush of a violent wind swept through the whole house."

In both John's and Luke's accounts of the Holy Spirit's coming, wind and breath are signs of the Spirit's presence. Luke emphasises the sound of the wind, perhaps because the sensory image of wind speaks strength and power. This sentence relates closely to the creation scene in the second verse of the Book of Genesis, where the author states, "the Earth was a formless void and darkness covered the face of the deep, while a wind from God swept over the face of the waters (Gn. 1:2). In new birth, it is wind, breeze, or breath – whatever you want to call it – that brings life.

In Acts, wind was the sign of renewed life coming to the Christian community, life that also came as tongues of fire, giving new speech and energy to the disciples. The power of the tongues of fire illustrates the power of the words of the preaching disciples. They moved from fear to confidence as powerful preachers of the Good News. Were John and Luke announcing the beginning of a new creation, or a new kingdom? In both stories Luke and John tell us that tremendous changes took place once the Holy Spirit came upon the community. In the "coming of the Spirit" narratives, John and Luke relate the story of the re-creation of the cosmos. At Pentecost the new age begins with the inauguration of the Church by the Spirit.

In Acts, "Divided tongues, as of fire, appeared with the wind, and a tongue of fire rested on each of the disciples." (Acts 1:3). Then the disciples emerged from their hiding place and began preaching fearlessly the Good News of Jesus. People of every nation heard them speak, each in his or her own tongue. It was the Spirit behind the words spoken so enthusiastically that set the fire of love ablaze in both the preachers and their listeners.

The Holy Spirit is not only Love, but also the Breath of Life. Metaphorically, the Holy Spirit is the breath that keeps on breathing. In and out, in and out, the breath of God breathes life into everything. The breath through which the Holy Spirit first breathed divine life into humankind continues to breathe new life now and forever. People – all people – are the Spirit's daughters and sons. We too breathe holy love in and out and in and out. The breath of the Spirit fills our hearts and recreates us by inviting us to embrace love.

When we, as Church, are at our best, we praise and glorify God through poetry or song, or story. All prayer is praise, but poetry carries the fullness of human love. Words of praise and glory are never just factual. Bare facts rarely communicate affection, reverence, and deep love. The Israelites knew this. They knew that the Genesis story began with images of strength and love. "In the beginning," wrote the author, "when God created the Heavens and the Earth, the Earth was a formless void and darkness covered the face of the deep, while a wind from God swept over the face of the waters. (Gn. 1:1-2)

The cosmos did not just come into being. Metaphorically, "a wind from God swept over the face of the waters." This wind initiated the fullness of light. The Pentecost story, like the creation story, is a love story.

The Bible is full of love stories. The whole of the Hebrew Scriptures is the story of the steadfastness of God's love for the Israelites, even when they are unfaithful. Individuals like David wrote love poems and songs in the psalms. Naomi loved Ruth. Jonathan loved David. In the Gospels Matthew, Mark, Luke, and John wrote love stories about Jesus. Paul handed over to his churches hymns of praise and love which Christians still sing today.

Veni Creator Spiritus

One of two great religious hymns of all time was written in the 9th Century: *Veni Creator Spiritus*. And the other is *Veni Sancte Spiritus*, written more than a millennium after Jesus' resurrection. Both are love poems. Each has been sung for centuries. Together they are poems that remind Christians everywhere of the Gift and gifts of the Holy Spirit.

Veni Creator Spiritus is an intimate song of faith, full of hope, and rich in love. The hymn is made up of an introductory verse, five verses describing the character and qualities of the Holy Spirit, and a closing doxology. It was written in Latin by Hrabanus Maurus in the 9th Century. He was then Abbot of the Benedictine monastery of Fulda, a monastery that became a centre of the arts and learning, famous throughout Europe.

Veni Creator Spiritus is a hymn of praise and a work of art. It lifts a single voice or a choir of many voices above themselves as they proclaim the glory of the Holy Spirit. This hymn is like a sublime Hebrew psalm. If one word carries its theme it is the word "come". "Come" is like Polaris, the North Star, the brightest star in the Ursa Minor constellation. "Come," sing the people in inviting the Holy Spirit. "Come," take your rest in us. "Come, Creator Spirit," bless all of creation with your presence and gifts. Following the invitation to "come" is a litany-like prayer naming the qualities and characteristics of the Holy Spirit:

Veni, Creator Spiritus,
mentes tuorum visita,
imple superna gratia
quae tu creasti pectora.
Qui diceris Paraclitus,
altissimi donum Dei,
fons vivus, ignus, caritas,
et spiritalis unctio.

Tu septiformis munere,
digitus paternae dexterae,
Tu rite promissum Patris,
sermone ditans guttura.

Accende lumen sensibus
infunde amorem cordibus:
infirma nostri corporis
virtute firmans perpeti.

Hostem repellas longius,
pacemque dones protinus:
ductore sic Te praevio
vitemus omne noxium.

Per Te sciamus da Patrem,
noscamus atque Filium;
Teque utriusque Spiritum
credamus omni tempore.

Deo Patri sit gloria,
et Filio, qui a mortuis
surrexit, ac Paraclito,
in saeculorum saecula.
Amen.

Come, Holy Spirit, Creator blest,
and in our souls take up Thy rest;
come with Thy grace and heavenly aid
to fill the hearts which Thou hast made.
O comforter, to Thee we cry,
O heavenly gift of God Most High,
O fount of life and fire of love,
and sweet anointing from above.

Thou in Thy sevenfold gifts are known;
Thou, finger of God's hand we own.
Thou, promise of the Father, Thou
Who dost the tongue with power imbue.

Kindle our senses from above,
and make our hearts o'erflow with love
with patience firm and virtue high
the weakness of our flesh supply.

Far from us drive the foe we dread,
and grant us Thy peace instead;
so shall we not, with Thee for guide,
turn from the path of life aside.

Oh, may Thy grace on us bestow
the Father and the Son to know;
and Thee, in endless times confessed,
of both the eternal Spirit blest.

Now to the Father and the Son,
Who rose from death, be glory given,
with Thou, O Holy Comforter,
henceforth by all in Earth and Heaven.
Amen.

In this hymn the singers name and describe the Holy Spirit as blessed creator, giver of grace, and as the comforter who is heavenly gift, the fount of life, and the fire of love.

> The singers beg the Spirit
> to kindle our senses,
> to make our hearts o'erflow with love,
> to supply or fill up our weakness,
> to drive our foes away,
> to grant us thy peace,
> and to be our guide.

Veni Creator Spiritus is a hymn not only for the feast of Pentecost but for every significant occasion of Christian life. It has always been sung before the beginning of an ecumenical council, the election of a pope, the consecration of a church, the profession of religious vows, and by small and large communities in times of special need. It is prayed in small group settings where communities come together to solve problems or plan initiatives for which they know they need the help of the Holy Spirit. In the United States parish councils sometimes begin their meetings with this prayer, which is an abbreviated form of the *Veni Creator Spiritus* hymn:

> *"Come Holy Ghost, creator blest,*
> *and in our hearts take up thy rest.*
> *Come with thy grace and heavenly aid,*
> *to fill the hearts which thou hast made".*

Veni Sancte Spiritus

Stephen Langton, the Archbishop of Canterbury, is said to have written the hymn *Veni Sancte Spiritus* in the early 13th Century. Just as the early Christians wrote hymns with glorious images of Christ, Langton wrote *Veni Sancte Spiritus* as a love poem with tender and strong images of Spirit-Love. Langton desired that the hymn would be sung on Pentecost Sunday and during the octave days of Pentecost.

Veni Sancte Spiritus describes in ten stanzas the different gifts Spirit-Love brings to the community. Chanting the poem in Latin was, even for those who did not understand the Latin, a wondrous experience. The sounds – chant and poetry – together spoke of beauty. In every line, for ten three-line stanzas, the grand and tender love of the Holy Spirit was heard through the voices of those who sang the hymn.

Veni Sancte Spiritus is a sequence, that is, a series or repetition of related characteristics. A sequence is like a group of numbers named in a related way, playing cards named in order of their power, or children named in the order of their birth. In this sequence *Veni Sancte Spiritus* the singers praise and glorify Spirit-Love for the Spirit's gifts to the people. This sequence sings of gifts that differ from those of *Veni Creator*. It names as gifts of Spirit-love the following:

verse 1   your radiant light
verse 2   yourself as giver of gifts
verse 3   greatest comforter,
verse 4   In work, comfort sweet
verse 5   Your love for humankind
verse 6   your grace
verse 7   cleanse the unclean
verse 8   fire that which is chilled
verse 9   your sevenfold gifts
verse 10   your eternal joy

Veni Sancte Spiritus

Veni, Sancte Spiritus,
et emitte caelitus
lucis tuae radium.
Veni, pater pauperum,
veni, dator munerum
veni, lumen cordium.

Come Holy Spirit,
send forth the heavenly
radiance of your light
Come, father of the poor,
come, giver of gifts,
come, light of the heart.

Consolator optime,
dulcis hospes animae,
dulce refrigerium.

Greatest comforter,
sweet guest of the soul,
sweet consolation.

In labore requies,
in aestu temperies
in fletu solatium.

In labour, rest,
in heat, temperance,
in tears, solace.

O lux beatissima,
reple cordis intima
tuorum fidelium.

O most blessed light,
fill the inmost heart
of your faithful.

Sine tuo numine,
nihil est in homine,
nihil est innoxium.

Without your light,
there is nothing in humans,
nothing that is pure.

Lava quod est sordidum,
riga quod est aridum,
sana quod est devium.
Flecte quod est rigidum,
fove quod est frigidum,
rege quod est devium.

Cleanse that which is unclean,
water that which is dry,
heal that which is wounded.
Bend that which is inflexible,
fire that which is chilled,
correct what goes astray.

Da tuis fidelibus,
in te confidentibus,
sacrum septenarium.

Give to your faithful,
those who trust in you,
the sevenfold gifts.

Da virtutis meritum,
Da salutis exitum,
da perenne gaudium,
Amen. Alleluia

Grant the reward of virtue,
grant the deliverance of salvation,
grant eternal joy.
Amen. Alleluia

In *Veni Sancte Spiritus* the petitioners seek for a response to specific human needs. The hymn names a sequence of both ordinary and great requests that people seek for from the Holy Spirit. The gifts of the Spirit are not extravagant gifts but loving responses to human needs. The petitioners address the Holy Spirit as "the giver of gifts," who responds to simple needs of the people with the gifts of rest, solace, and light.

Veni Sancte Spiritus is a hymn of petition. The musical form is simple chant. With many vowels and flowing rhythm, this Latin hymn has a soft, gentle sound. The hymn-prayer is a work of love in which each rhyming line with seven syllables sets forth the needs of people for the Spirit's gifts. The melody and text move seamlessly from people's needs to a sequence of gifts in response to the needs.

In the first four stanzas the praying community calls on the Holy Spirit to "come." There is an intensity, almost an anxiety, in that call. "Come," is repeated three times in the second stanza alone. Whenever the community prays to the Holy Spirit, it calls in a compelling way: COME! The other, much older hymn, *Veni Creator Spiritus*, begins with the same compelling phrase, "Come, Creator Spirit."

The word "come" is not only compelling, expressing the community's ardent desire and need for the Spirit, but it demonstrates the profound relationship that exists between those who love and count on the Spirit and those whom the Spirit loves. We cannot be separated, the call says. "Come, we are in need of you."

A second characteristic of the first four stanzas of the *Veni Sancte Spiritus* is the different way in which the praying community names the Spirit. The Spirit is the "Holy Spirit," "Father of the poor," "giver of gifts," "light of the heart." In later verses the prayer names the Holy Spirit "greatest comforter," "sweet guest of the soul," "sweet consolation," "most blessed light." These titles express intimacy and confidence in the Holy Spirit.

A third remarkable characteristic of the *Veni Sancte Spiritus* is the acknowledgement of the ordinary yet intimate gifts the people ask from the Spirit.

Stanza one:	the radiance of your light;
Stanza four:	rest, soothing coolness, solace;
Stanza five:	fill the inmost heart of your faithful;
Stanza seven:	cleanse what is unclean,
	heal what is wounded;
Stanza eight:	bend the inflexible,
	heat what is cold;
	correct what is astray;
Stanza nine:	the sevenfold gifts;
Stanza ten:	the reward of virtue,
	salvation and eternal joy.

In this profound yet simple prayer the prayers exhibit humility, simplicity, and a deeply personal love of the Holy Spirit. The prayers do not ask for worldly gifts or revenge against enemies, or rewards for goodness. They seek simple gifts. They are passionate lovers, handing themselves over to the One they trust. It is not so much that they think about what to ask for. They simply ask for what their hearts deeply desire.

There is an ethereal quality in the relationship between the musical rhythm and the verbal text, between the worshippers and the Holy Spirit. The worshippers are Christians who know the Spirit as the one who lives within them who seeks their welfare, loves them with tenderness, energises them with Spirit life and a sense of reverence toward the mystery of the Spirit. The hymn *Veni Sancte Spiritus* voices a plea for all kinds of gifts from Spirit-Love but always with an underlying spirit of confidence in the Spirit's generosity. We can almost hear the singers singing in their hearts, *"You are our Spirit-Love, we are your beloveds. We love you always."* It is as if the Spirit breathed her breath within them and they in turn sing out of that very breath.

The Spirit to whom 13th Century Christians sang is the same Spirit who breathes on us. We live in and through the same Spirit who continues to brings new life and gifts of wisdom, knowledge, peace, counsel, courage, piety, and fear of the Lord. The gifts of the Spirit are characteristics of the Spirit's love. They give us strength and courage to meet all our needs.

The Holy Spirit's love enables us to breathe one breath after another without ceasing. God's love never grows cold, or stale, or boring, and with the Holy Spirit's love, our breathing becomes so peaceful that we almost forget living is going on, steadily, for years and years. People grow old without consciously realising that every time they pray silently to the Spirit from the heart, they are growing closer to one another and to Trinity, the source of all relationships and mission.

Stephen Langton called on the Spirit to come and be with us, to bring radiant light. Langton recognised the Spirit's action and relationship in human life. "Come," he continued, calling the Holy Spirit, "the father of the poor," all of us who are poor but who become rich with love.

"Come giver of gifts, Come, light of the heart, (...)

Come, our comforter, our guest, our consolation." "You are," sing the faithful to the Spirit, "rest in our labour," "temperance" in our heat, "solace" in our tears. You are "the blessed light" that fills "our inmost heart." Those who sing know that without the Spirit's light there is "nothing left in humanity, nothing that is pure."

Images of the Spirit-Love in the Two Medieval Hymns

These two hymns share many images of the Spirit. They also share chant music, though musicians have written other forms of music to accompany the texts. It may be possible that the power and energy of the Holy Spirit was recognised more fully in a time when an archbishop could write such a hymn, and during the seven centuries in which great composers continued to write new music to accompany and support the text of these great Spirit hymns. And we continue to sing beautiful hymnody today, in small churches, in hidden places, and in cathedrals. Occasionally we even sing to the Spirit.

In these two hymns descriptions of the Holy Spirit differ radically from most images of the Father and the Son. They are more poetic, more pastoral. The singers ask the Spirit to bring forth "radiant light." They describe the Spirit as "rest in labour," "solace in tears," indicating gentleness and love rather than power or might. The Holy Spirit is the one who "heals" and is the very "light of the heart." The hymns burst with energetic love while they also are also full of peace and tenderness.

Every action of the Spirit is an act of love, and this

love relates the people who sing of love with one another and with the Spirit. The singers describe themselves as "your faithful," and "those who trust in you." They ask the Spirit for "humble gifts," gifts for which marginalised and suffering people might long, gifts that loving and poor people would seek. The hymns are full of love for all people, but perhaps primarily for those who are often forgotten by their own communities.

The images of the Holy Spirit in both hymns suggest ways in which the Spirit loves both the community and the individual. The texts are simple and clear. The love of the Holy Spirit is a constant theme throughout the texts. In fact, the gentleness of Spirit-Love permeates the text. I say "permeates" because the hymns are full of balanced and reciprocal movement. They are hymns of pure love. Each hymn has a passionate tone, calling for a response to needs. *Veni Sancte Spiritus* notes plaintively that "without your light," there is "nothing in humanity, nothing that is pure."

These two hymns, the *Veni Creator Spiritus* and the *Veni Sancte Spiritus,* offer us an abundance of fresh images of the Holy Spirit. One could think that the Spirit might be the most difficult of the persons in Trinity to name, but the images of the Spirit given in these two hymns are amazing in what they tell us about how the Christian faith community related to the Spirit centuries ago.

Spirit-Love is traditionally referred to in feminine form as if she is a mother, and in this maternal image becomes intimately close to those who sing these hymns. The singers/prayers ask the Holy Spirit to bring peace, grace, healing, gifts, rest, and comfort, "to fill the hearts which thou has made," "deliver salvation and eternal joy." These words express an intimacy of love, a personal familiarity, an openness and freedom of speech that comes only from the experience of mutual love. The Holy Spirit is not a distant stranger – Spirit-Love is a healing and deeply loving friend.

Spirit-Love relates to ordinary labourers and to hardworking mothers who give themselves in and through difficult work for their families. In the world of Mystery, the poor always seem to be favoured by the Holy Spirit. Perhaps it was only the clergy or trained choirs who could sing these hymns in Latin, but everyone who heard them sung as an act of love would hear the echoes of otherworldly sounds of the chant in which they were sung. These hymns emerged from love and they expressed a deep love for the Spirit-Love; they beseech the Spirit to "enkindle the fire of your love" in us – both singers and listeners.

Who is the God we Love?

In his first letter to the Corinthians, Paul wrote a description of love that includes many forms of ordinary daily human actions. Each action is good in itself, but the actions gathered together offer one harmonious description of love.

Love is patient;
love is kind;
love is not envious or boastful or arrogant or rude.
Love does not insist on its own way;
it is not irritable or resentful;
it does not rejoice in wrongdoing,
but rejoices in the truth.
It bears all things,
believes all things,
hopes all things,
endures all things.

– (1Cor. 13:4-7)

This Pauline description of Christian love, glorious as it may be, does not begin to describe Trinity's love, for no words or images can ever fully describe divine Love. The God Christians love is Trinity, and Trinity's love far exceeds even the beauty of the human love that Paul describes.

Some Christians ask, "Who is Trinity?" "What is Trinity like?" "How does Trinity relate to us?" "Can we relate to Trinity?" "What does it mean to say God is Trinity?" "What difference does Trinity really make in our lives?"

As noted earlier, it was Jesus who introduced us to Trinity, speaking of God as "the Father, the Son, and the Holy Spirit." Over centuries Christians developed an understanding of God through their daily living, their membership in the Church, through prayer and study. Theologians, mystics, martyrs, and leaders of the Church explained that the one divine Holy Being is three persons, three equal, related, and differentiated persons who are one in Love.

Trinitarian love flows as a resplendent ocean of love, always giving birth to new love in every creative form. Love flows from Trinity as alive and magnetic. The love that reaches out from Trinity emerges from the Lover, the Beloved, and Spirit-Love who is the Love that unites all of creation as one loving beloved.

Love is never an isolated action. Love is always relational. Love expresses relatedness through free and mutual self-giving. The Mystery of Trinitarian Love is, first of all, that it is so full, energetic, and enlivening that it constantly gives birth to new love. Trinity lives and loves through the energy of Spirit-Love. Spirit-Love is creative and so passionate that it is beyond our understanding. It can only be accepted and received like true friendship – through openness and humility. Spirit-Love is pure gift.

In the beginning Spirit-Love expressed itself lovingly through creating. In loving that which it brought into being, it gave and elicited, gives and elicits, love in return. It continued and continues to bring forth newness. It was a rather short time ago, only a few millennia, when the Israelites recognise God's pattern of interaction with them and the refrain that permeated their sacred Scriptures told all who would listen that "God is steadfast in love." The Israelites acknowledged that they were not steadfast in their love, but even with their faithlessness they proclaimed that "God is steadfast in love." That refrain could be considered as the primary theme of the Hebrew Scriptures. The Israelites' commitment in faith led them to tell the story of God's love and even as they praised and glorified the God of Love, other peoples discovered God's love in their own ways.

It was Jesus who through his life-death-resurrection and preaching revealed the nature of Trinity's love for all peoples. Jesus' final admonition to his disciples to preach to all nations was a public proclamation of Trinity's love for all. Trinity who lived as Love before the beginning loves us who are creatures of divine Love. This is a mystery, but mystery is never unfathomable, or totally unknown. Mystery is that which we can never fully know or understand. At the same time it is that which we can always continue to understand in a new way. The mystery of the Trinity is the mystery of the God of Love who loves all people and all creation ever more fully, and who invites all to participate in divine life and love.

To know God is not easy, for it is not easy to speak of or about God who is spirit, unseen except indirectly through beauty and love. Nothing anyone says about love is ever adequate, though "God is Love" is one of the most transforming sentences in the world.

For us, loving is a human art. It begins with the experience of being loved and is shared by touching, embracing, speaking, singing, hearing, and seeing. Love is shared primarily through the art of speaking, the art of music, the art of creating beauty, the art of dance. Love is sensual, coming into the heart through touching and through all the senses. Yet it is the energy of Spirit-love that ties us to divine love and enables us to relate to the One who is, in essence, the fullness of love.

To recognise and respond to Trinitarian love is to be one with Trinity. Through the act of responding, which is itself a divine gift, people share in the beauty and harmony of divine life. Trinitarian life is not a gift we await. It is already here. It enables us to be patient and kind, neither envious nor boastful nor arrogant nor rude. To be one with God who *is* love, who is loving, and who lives within us is to be transformed. That God is one in love and that God loves us is what Jesus came to tell and show us by his words and his actions.

Trinity is a community of dynamic love always moving beyond itself in love to others. That which unites the love partners is Spirit-Love, the mutual giving and accepting of divine Love. In love and through love Trinity gives birth to all that is. In her book, *God For Us,* Catherine Mowry LaCugna wrote that Trinity tells us that God is "essentially relational, ecstatic, fecund, alive as passionate love." She goes on to say that "the doctrine of the Trinity is ultimately ... a teaching not about the abstract nature of God, but a teaching about God's life with us and our life with each other."

Through our experiences of Spirit-love – through the Church as the Mystery of Christ incarnate and through the love of others – Trinity reveals to us who we are as human beings and who we are invited to be. Trinity tells us that we are meant to be a loving community as the Trinity is a loving communion. To be a loving community, each member of the community must be not only loving but also accepting of the love of others. Knowing that the Triune God is love itself gives us extraordinary insight into our own humanity. The foundational belief of Christian faith is that *God is Love* (Jn 4:8).

For the moment, discard whatever it is that hides your view of God and consider what faith and hope and love can mean in your life. "Faith" is not blind acceptance of unintelligible intellectual concepts. In biblical language the word "faith" names a person or a community's *commitment of love* in response to God's love. The word "hope" does not mean unreasonable expectations, but total trust in the God experienced as goodness. Being loved by God is an experience of intimate union with the God whom we name Love. God's love calls for our response of love. Faith, hope, and love are ways of being human, lifting us up beyond ourselves to be one with each other and one with God.

Recognising God as a loving Trinity enables human beings to sing and dance and live with deep delight. Appreciating the depth and breadth of God's love not only for us, but for all that is, lifts up our hearts. Encouraged by being loved compels us to embrace lovingly what God loves, and we become ever more closely related in love.

Through love we are one divine-human family. Through love and reverence for all of creation we are one with all of creation. The whole universe—the cosmos--is God's symbol of Trinitarian love.

> *Love never ends. But as for prophecies, they will come to an end; as for tongues, they will cease; as for knowledge, it will come to an end. For we know only in part, and we prophesy only in part; but when the complete comes, the partial will come to an end (...) For now we see in a mirror, dimly, but then we will see face to face. Now I know only in part; then I will know fully, even as I have been fully known. And now faith, hope, and love abide, these three; and the greatest of these is love.*
>
> – (1Cor. 12:13)

FIVE

BEING ONE IN LOVE

Jesus' Last Supper Discourse

The apostle John was known as the "beloved disciple," or we could say that John was Jesus' "best friend." It is reasonable to assume that because of their friendship John could and did express Jesus' thoughts in a clearer and fuller way than did the other evangelists. John's version of the Last Supper discourse (John: Ch. 13-17) is more complete than those of the other evangelists. The details are fuller, richer, and more personal. In writing his account, John uses the tone of a friend: admiring, loving, deeply personal. He tells his reader in detail about Jesus' actions at the Last Supper, and he uses Jesus' own words to disclose the depth of Jesus' relationship with his disciples as well as with the Father and the Holy Spirit.

John's Gospel is both lengthy and lyrical. It was written near the end of the 1st Century CE. It begins with a prologue-poem of extraordinary beauty in which John, with just a few lines, connects the whole of the Jewish tradition with the heart of Christian life. John is not only a "beloved disciple," he is also a theologian. Chapters one through twelve, known as the Book of Signs, introduce the reader to the life and ministry of Jesus. Chapters 13-21 are called the Book of Glory because they describe the glorification of Jesus beginning with the Last Supper and progress through his suffering, death, and resurrection, culminating with his heavenly glorification.

The remarkable Prologue to this Gospel is not only a loving and exalted introduction to Jesus as God's Son, but is also a classic work of literary art in which John glorifies Jesus as the "beloved Son of God," and "the Word made flesh." The beginning words of John's Gospel are startling, for this gospel begins with the same words as the opening of the Book of Genesis. With this beginning John connects the beginning of creation with the beginning of the Christian era:

> *In the beginning was the Word, and the Word was with God, and the Word was God. He was in the beginning with God. All things came into being, through him, and without him not one thing came into being. What has come into being in him was life, and the life was the light of all people. The light shines in the darkness, and the darkness did not overcome it.*
>
> *– Jn 1:1-5*

Later in the Prologue, John goes on to say that

He [Jesus] was in the world, and the world came into being through him; yet the world did not know him. He came to what was his own, and his own people did not accept him. But to all who received him, who believed in his name, he gave power to become children of God, who were born, not of blood or of the will of the flesh or of the will of man, but of God. And the Word became flesh and lived among us, and we have seen his glory, the glory as of a father's only son, a full of grace and truth.

On the night before he died, Jesus gathered with his apostles in an upper room for what would come to be called the Last Supper. John describes the Last Supper events in Chapters 13-17 of his Gospel. He vividly describes Jesus' words and actions, and in the end he acknowledges his own role as the disciple Jesus loved, saying,

[24] *his is* [I am] *the disciple who is testifying to these things and has written them, and we know that his testimony is true.*

John's Gospel differs broadly from the other three gospels because of this special relationship. As a beloved friend, John treasured Jesus' words and they remained in his heart. John wrote as a friend about his friend. It is for this reason that John's Gospel is so eloquent, nuanced, and loving.

"Abide in Me" Chapter 15: 1-17

Chapter 15, the *Abide in Me* chapter, is the centre and the heart of the Last Supper discourse. In it Jesus reveals more about himself, his values, and his loves than he does in any other discourse. The whole chapter is a commentary on Jesus' understanding of friendship. It is a personal revelation not only about his friendship-love of the Lover/ Father and the Spirit/Love, but also of his relationship with other human beings, one of whom carefully remembered what Jesus had to say about friendship:

I am the true vine, and my Father is the vine grower. He removes every branch in me that bears no fruit. Every branch that bears fruit he prunes to make it bear more fruit. You have already been cleansed by the word that I have spoken to you. Abide in me as I abide in you. Just as the branch cannot bear fruit by itself unless it abides in the vine, neither can you unless you abide in me. I am the vine, you are the branches. Those who abide in me and I in them bear much fruit, because apart from me you can do nothing. 6 Whoever does not abide in me is thrown away like a branch and withers; such branches are gathered, thrown into the fire, and burned. If you abide in me, and my words abide in you, ask for whatever you wish, and it will be done for you. My Father is glorified by this, that you bear much fruit and become my disciples. As the Father has loved me, so I have loved you; abide in my love. If you keep my commandments, you will abide in my love, just as I have kept my Father's commandments and abide in his love. I have said these things to you so that my joy may be in you, and that your joy may be complete.

This is my commandment, that you love one another as I have loved you. No one has greater love than this, to lay down one's life for one's friends. You are my friends if you do what I command you. I do not call you servants any longer, because the servant does not know what the master is doing; but I have called you friends, because I have made known to you everything that I have heard from my Father. You did not choose me but I chose you. And I appointed you to go and bear fruit, fruit that will last, so that the Father will give you whatever you ask him in my name. I am giving you these commands so that you may love one another.

Chapter 15 begins with Jesus speaking in a radical and unequivocal way about the closeness of his relationship with the apostles. He speaks solemnly and poetically of his love for these disciples. Using the metaphor of the vine and the branches to stand for his relationship with them, Jesus speaks of the intimacy they shared. Jesus describes their relationship as an "indwelling" or an "abiding" with one another. He repeats "Abide in me," or some form of it, ten times in six short verses.

Abide in me *as I abide in you. Just as the branch cannot bear fruit by itself unless it* abides in the vine, *neither can you unless* you abide in me. *I am the vine, you are the branches. Those who* abide in me *and* I in them *bear much fruit, because apart from me you can do nothing. Whoever does not* abide in me *is thrown away like a branch and withers; such branches are gathered, thrown into the fire, and burned. If you* abide in me, *and my words* abide in you, *ask for whatever you wish, and it will be done for you.*

These verses reveal the depth of Jesus' personal relationship with his apostles. He sees himself not as their "Lord" and "master," but as their friend. He actually says:

[9] *As the Father has loved me, so I have loved you;* abide *in my love.*

He professes his deep love for these ordinary men – fishermen, labourers, husbands, fathers, and even Judas. John may be Jesus' best friend, but Jesus invites all of the apostles into a personal friendship-love with him.

Jesus, in professing his love for the apostles, asks for their friendship in return. "Abide in me," Jesus says. The word "abide" is not a commonly used word in today's culture. The translation of the Bible used in this book (the *New Revised Standard Version*) uses the word "abide." However, other translators use different terms. The *Anchor*

Bible translates the Greek word as "remain," in the phrase, "Remain in me". The *New American Bible* translates the same Greek word as "live," as "Live in me". Raymond E. Brown, scholar and translator of the Gospel of John in the *Anchor Bible* series, pointed out that he translated "Abide in me" as "Remain in me," because that word harmonised more closely with the original verb tense and meaning. The word "remain" records the reality that Jesus was not issuing an invitation to a new friendship; he publicly acknowledges an already existing relationship. Jesus urges the apostles to continue to grow in friendship with him even as he acknowledges his own friendship for them.

The apostles were a common lot, unusual only in their devotion to Jesus as their Lord and master. Now, at the Last Supper, everything about their relationship with Jesus was changing, and they may have been bewildered at what was happening. On this night, the night before he died, Jesus spoke to them of friendship, saying not only that he was their friend but that the Father/Lover also was their friend and desired their friendship in return.

After Jesus spoke of abiding in them, he told them that they were to love one another and all others as he loved them. Perhaps he was preparing them for his death, for this seems to be a call to a new way of life. Jesus told them that his Father was glorified by them and loved them as he, Jesus, did. This may have been a startling, maybe even frightening revelation to them:

⁸ My Father is glorified by this, that you bear much fruit and become my disciples. ⁹ As the Father has loved me, so I have loved you; abide in my love. *¹⁰ If you keep my commandments, you will* abide in my love, *just as I have kept my Father's commandments and* abide in his love. *¹¹ My Father is glorified by this, that you bear much fruit and become my disciples.*

On this evening, with Jesus' profession of the Father's love for the apostles and his gift of the Father's commandment of love to the apostles, everything changed. The kingdom was becoming. At this point everything must have looked very different from the past. The apostles would still need time to absorb what they had heard. The apostles probably had no idea of what belonging to this new community of love involved. Eventually each of them would commit himself in his own way to friendship with Jesus and through him with the Father and the Spirit and the community. Everything changed.

Throughout the Last Supper discourse Jesus speaks to his apostles of his closeness in love with the Father and the Spirit. He professes his love for the Father and the Spirit as well as his love for them. He warns them that he will be going away from them to the Father, and he indicates that afterwards he will send the Spirit to them. They would never be left alone. Jesus also tells the apostles that his Father has many "mansions" or "dwelling places," and that he will go to prepare a place for them. Jesus gave his apostles hope by promising to bring them to the place where he and the Father would be.

Jesus' words powerfully declare his union of love with the Father and the Spirit, and also clearly express his deep friendship-love for those who shared supper with him: "*I do not call you servants, but friends.*"The "*Abide in me*"talk reveals God reaching out through Jesus to his apostles and through them to all God's people. We are meant to be a people who are intimately related through love. Indeed, all of creation is a universe of love.

I Call You Friends (15:12-17)

In the last part of the *Abide in Me* discourse, Jesus speaks about his friendship with his apostles:

> [12] *This is my commandment, that you love one another as I have loved you.*
> [13] *No one has greater love than this, to lay down one's life for one's* friends. [14] *You are my* friends *if you do what I command you.* [15] *I do not call you servants any longer, because the servant does not know what the master is doing; but I have called you* friends, *because I have made known to you everything that I have heard from my Father.* 16 *You did not choose me but I chose you. And I appointed you to go and bear fruit, fruit that will last, so that the Father will give you whatever you ask him in my name.* [17] *I am giving you these commands so that you may love one another.*

Jesus' words are straightforward and powerful. First, he commands his followers in a startling way to love one another – as he loves them. He makes clear the depth of his love: *"No one has greater love than this, to lay down one's life for one's friends."* His awareness of imminent death brings solemnity to his words.

> [14] *You are my friends if you do what I command you,*

Jesus says, and as if to emphasise his friendship, he assures them of his love, saying,

> [15] *I do not call you servants any longer because the servant does not know what the master is doing; but I have called you friends, because I have made known to you everything that I have heard from my Father. Abide in me... You are my friends if you do what I command you. I call you friends; you did not choose me but I chose you. Love one another.*

Perhaps Jesus presumed that after this supper discourse the disciples might respond to his love by supporting him, or they might gather around him protecting him from whatever might happen. Whatever Jesus hoped for, only one apostle stood with the women at the foot of the cross on the following day. It seems the others were not yet ready to act as his friends.

One could read the entire "Abide in Me" discourse from many different perspectives. We can read it in order to understand what Jesus was asking of his friends. Or we might ask, "What is Jesus telling us about ourselves?" or "What is he telling us about God's love?" or "Why did he repeat again and again that we are to 'love one another'?"

Friendship is pure gift. It is a love that is mutually given and mutually accepted. No one can earn it, lend it, borrow it, buy it, or take it away. *"You did not choose me, I chose you."* The wonder of this gift is that Trinity offers friendship to all people in all times. As followers of Jesus in the 21st Century we, too, have been invited to participate in divine friendship. Created in the image and likeness of Trinity, we relate to Trinity in response to Trinity's choice of us. It is the nature of Trinity to love and to accept love.

Who is the God We Love?

Jesus, speaking about Trinity, gave the first Christians images that revealed the nature of Trinity and enabled those Christians to name God – an action that the Jewish people hesitated to do. Their relationship to the God of Israel was so reverent that they would not speak God's name. The unpronounceable YWWH was their indirect way of naming God.

Jesus named God "Father," "Son," and "Holy Spirit," and since his time Christians have so named the Triune God. From the beginning of the Church's history, Christians have proclaimed the Triune God every time they prayed.

They begin and end their prayer, "In the name of the Father, the Son and the Holy Spirit". Christians baptise, confirm, marry, and bury in that same name. We forgive sins in the name of the Father, the Son, and the Holy Spirit, and when we celebrate Eucharist we return again and again to proclaim and give thanks in the name of the Father, the Son, and the Holy Spirit. Christians are a Trinitarian people.

But there is a problem with these images of Trinity. Perhaps the Jews are wiser in not attempting to name God. As a Jew, Jesus knew that God was spirit without gender, even though Jews often used male images for God: king, shepherd, father, sower, judge, warrior. Eventually they began to act on the concept of males being "more like God," separating the women from the men, giving the men authority because of their gender. In so doing, women became subject to males, sometimes mere objects that could be sold or bartered. And in Christian cultures, women came to have only the value that men gave to them.

Today, in a society becoming ever more aware of the value of women in themselves, the words Jesus used to name Trinity seem offensive to many women and men. But we can change our images, while still giving praise to Trinity. To do nothing is to continue to oppress women. To do away with exclusively male imagery would make our Church stronger and more loving, and our prayer more authentic. It may take a long time to remove the stigma against women evident in male imagery. In the Roman Catholic Church, for example, women still have no official participation in Church leadership on any level above an associate pastor in a parish.

One way to initiate change would be to use the formula of the Trinity suggested in the 4th Century by St Augustine. Using his words, we could say, "Glory be to our Lover, our Beloved, and the Love who unifies us." Or we could say, "In the name of our Lover, and of our Beloved, and of the Spirit of Love." These Augustinian terms are deeply relational and best identify the nature of the Trinity we worship. With them, Trinity is praised, and our prayer would clearly reflect the reality that women and men are equal children of God.

Images remain problematic, for Trinity can never be adequately described in human terms. John the beloved apostle stated simply that "God is love," and that is probably the best we can do.

Trinity is Mystery

We simply cannot find any one understanding of Trinity better than "Trinity is Love". Trinity-love informs all our human loves and life's mysteries. Friendship is a mystery. Parental love is a mystery. Spousal love is mystery. Trinity is profound mystery, beyond human comprehension, yet Trinity-love invites humankind to join it in the act of loving so that we may be one in friendship with Trinity.

One of the most important doctrinal proclamations of the Second Vatican Council declares that:

"It pleased God, in his goodness and wisdom, to reveal

himself and to make known the mystery of his will (see Ephesians 1:9), which was that people can draw near to the Father, through Christ, the Word made flesh in the Holy Spirit, and thus become sharers in the divine nature (see Eph. 2:18; 2Pet 1:4). By this revelation, then, the invisible God (see Col. 1:15; 1Tim 1:17), from the fullness of his love, addresses men and women as his friends (See Ex 33:11; Jn 15:14-16; and lives among them (Bar 3:38) to invite and receive them into his own company." (*Dei Verbum*, art. 2, 965).

Even in this sparse language the heart of the Mystery shines through all that is and touches humankind both communally and individually.

Jesus led us to know Trinity through his ministry of preaching. As the Son, he told us about the Father and the Holy Spirit. St Augustine interpreted Jesus' words by writing of the Lover, the Beloved, and the unifying Love that makes the three one. But Trinity's love is not restricted to the inner life of God. Trinity reaches out in love to all of creation. The beauty, harmony, order, unity of creation are simply signs of Trinitarian love. Trinity is the fullness of love embracing us far beyond our deserving or understanding.

Trinity embraces all peoples of all ages. We do not know how divine love lives in us. We know we experience both loving and being loved. Throughout history saints and scholars have tried to name God, and we have not come near to naming the unnameable.

Trinity is Mystery. Friendship is a mystery. Relationships are a mystery. Life is a mystery. Love is a mystery. Yet we simply cannot identify any mystery that surpasses the mystery of Trinitarian Love. Trinitarian love is so deep, so expansive, so close and yet so distant, so timeless yet so immediate. Trinity calls us to love, takes away barriers to our loving, and surprises us. It is simply a story of faith and hope and Love. It is a story that began in the beginning, that is, and that continues. This story has no ending, and, ultimately, Trinity is a story of deep, deep delight. Alleluia!

References

The Scripture quotations contained herein are from the *Holy Bible*, New Revised Standard Version, Catholic Gift Edition: Anglicised Text. San Francisco: Harper Collins Publishers, 2007.

The New Oxford Annotated Bible with Apocrypha: New Revised Standard Version. Oxford University Press. Kindle Edition. Coogan, Michael D.; Brettler, Marc Z.; Perkins, Pheme; Newsom, Carol A. (2010-01-20).

Afterword

I need to say that I write about the Trinity because of the works of three great theologians, Dr Catherine Mowry LaCugna (1952-1997), formerly Professor of Theology at Notre Dame University; Dr Elizabeth A. Johnson, presently Distinguished Professor of Theology at Fordham University; and Leonardo Boff, a Latin American theologian who has enriched the Church with many eminently readable and transformative theology books and essays on the Trinity.

LaCugna stirred the love of the Trinity in my heart through her book, *God for Us*. In 1992, LaCugna introduced me to a God too big for me to wrap my arms around, yet loving enough for me to embrace. In that same decade, Professor Johnson wrote an essay entitled *TRINITY: To Let the Symbol Sing Again*, affirming that "the goal of all Creation is to participate in the Trinitarian mystery of love". Johnson challenged her readers "to let the symbol 'Trinity' sing again". I decided to take up her challenge, and, as best I could, let the Trinitarian symbol "sing again" in our time. Leonardo Boff wrote two books focusing on different aspects of Trinitarian life: *Holy Trinity, Perfect Community* (2000) and *Come Holy Spirit (2015)*. The first of those two books is short and theologically rich. Another Boff book, *The Cry of the Earth, the Cry of the Poor* emerges out of a Trinitarian perspective, and the Earth and the Poor are both alive within a Trinitarian context.

I recently found close resonance with the aim of Sarah Coakley's book, *God, Sexuality, and the Self: An Essay on the Trinity*. My hope for my own "story of deep delight" parallels her view that her book on the Triune God is "for all those who continue to seek a vision of God for today, one attractive enough to magnetise their deepest human longings".

Everything is related dynamically because Trinity is the living source of all life and love. Trinity is in itself a relationship of intimate love. 'Everything that is' is connected through the divine love that brought what is into existence.

ACKNOWLEDGEMENTS

Fortunately I am a member of a congregation of loving, faithful, and well educated women, my Sinsinawa Dominican sisters, who did not hesitate to assist me as I wrote this book. I thank them all. My overwhelming thanks go to Rita Claire Dorner, O.P., friend and colleague, for her critique of both the content and form of this writing. She read every paragraph several times, as only a friend will do, bringing to the readings her scholarship, her profound love of the arts, and her lived experience of faithful Catholic life.

Mary Paynter, O.P., offered to edit this writing, giving it a professional cast that preserved its spirit and gives a clarity that makes it whole. I also thank Mary for the wisdom, generosity, friendship and faith which accompanied her editing.

I offer gratitude also to Sisters Patricia Mulcahey, O.P., Mary Ellen Gevelinger, O.P., and Antoinette Harris, O.P., who as leaders in our congregation supported my work generously. Doris Rauenhorst, O.P., as Director of Study, encouraged and supported me. The assistance of Jeanette Landuyt, O.P., who tried to keep me organised has been invaluable. Without Greg Funk, our computer wizard, this book would never have come to print.

I also acknowledge Stephen A. Privett, S.J., colleague and friend, who constantly challenges my thinking and offers beneficial criticism as only a Jesuit friend can do.

Last but far from least, throughout the writing of this book my niece, Sheila McNulty Serafin, assisted in bringing this work to fruition by keeping my heart loving and my humour intact.